D0360488

# THE NEW DICTIONARY OF COUNTED-THREAD EMBROIDERY STITCHES

## Other Books by Rhoda Ochser Goldberg

*The New Knitting Dictionary*
*The New Crochet Dictionary*
*The New Quilting and Patchwork Dictionary*
*A New Dictionary of Quilt Designs in Cross-Stitch*
*The New Dictionary of Needlepoint & Canvas Stitches*
*Needlepoint Patterns for Signs and Sayings* (with Marion Pakula)

# THE NEW
# DICTIONARY OF COUNTED-THREAD EMBROIDERY STITCHES

## RHODA OCHSER GOLDBERG

THREE RIVERS PRESS • NEW YORK

Copyright © 1998 by Rhoda Ochser Goldberg

All rights reserved. No part of this book may be reproduced or transmitted in any form or by any means, electronic or mechanical, including photocopying, recording, or by any information storage and retrieval system, without permission in writing from the publisher.

Published by Three Rivers Press, a division of Crown Publishers, Inc., 201 East 50th Street, New York, New York 10022. Member of the Crown Publishing Group.

Random House, Inc. New York, Toronto, London, Sydney, Auckland
www.randomhouse.com

THREE RIVERS PRESS and colophon are trademarks of Crown Publishers, Inc.

Printed in the United States of America

Library of Congress Cataloging-in-Publication Data
  Goldberg, Rhoda Ochser.
    New dictionary of counted-thread embroidery stitches / Rhoda Ochser Goldberg. — 1st pbk. ed.
      p.   cm.
    1. Counted-thread embroidery—Dictionaries.  I. Title.
TT778.C65G56   1998
746.44'3'03—dc21                                                    97-15954
                                                                     CIP

ISBN 0-517-88663-4

10   9   8   7   6   5   4   3   2   1

First Edition

*This book is lovingly dedicated to my children, Alan and Jackie and Jacqui and Matt, and my grandchildren, Jason, Ryan, and Emily Rose.*

# Contents

# Acknowledgments

I gratefully acknowledge the support and assistance I received from my friends and family and the wonderful groups of stitchers who gave so freely of their time and talents. I would never have been able to produce a book of this scope and size without the help of these dedicated groups of women.

I must thank the members and officers of the Suffolk County and Long Island Chapters of the Embroiderers' Guild of America and the Canvas Fanatics Chapter of the American Needlepoint Guild for making the majority of the samples photographed for inclusion in this book.

A special word of gratitude and thanks must go to my friend Dale Sokolow for her help in suggesting stitchers, correcting instructions, stitching samples, and offering her helping hand whenever I asked for anything. Thank you again, Dale; you are a most talented person.

A special thank-you to the people of the needlecraft industry, who have always given of their time, knowledge, equipment, and products needed to make the samples for this book. This book could never have been written without their cooperation and assistance.

I will never write a book without acknowledging my first writing partner and teacher, Marion Pakula. Thank you again for showing me how to take a book from an idea into reality.

The photographs were provided by my friend Marilyn Lehrfeld. Your photographic ability will always keep me in awe of you. Thanks again, Marilyn.

Last but never least, the most important word of thanks goes to my editor, Brandt Aymar. He did his usual assistance and hand-holding, and above all encouraged me to keep writing about the needlecrafts I love so dearly. We will miss you.

## Samples were made by the following stitchers:

Lynn Bryan, Kings Park, New York
Pat Conway, Huntington, New York
Paula Comans, Rockville Center, New York
Karen De Rogatis, Carteret, New Jersey
Helena Dittmar, Jackson Heights, New York
Florence Fazekas, Bayside, New York
Jackie Goldberg, New York

Marilyn Goldberg, East Hampton, New York
Bobbie Graham, Levittown, New York
Gilda Hecht, Great Neck, New York
Rita Limback, Whitestone, New York
Betty Lombardi, Huntington, New York
Maxine Meyers, Dix Hills, New York
Anita Miller, Boca Raton, Florida

Jacqui O'Connell, Pensacola, Florida
Ruth O'Connell, Newton Square,
    Pennsylvania
Diane Pleines, Mamaroneck, New York

Marge Rogers, Sayville, New York
Dale Sokolow, Melville, New York
Margaret Vickary, Smithtown, New York
Eileen Weingaertner, Westbury, New York

**Materials and supplies for making the samples were generously provided by the following companies:**

**Bucilla®-Hazelton,** Pennsylvania (Ribband® by Bucilla®)

**C & L Crafts Co.,** Eugene, Oregon *(Color Caddy™)*

**Charles Craft,** Laurinburg, North Carolina *(towels, fiddlers cloth)*

**Dal-Craft, Inc.,** Tucker, Georgia *(magnetic boards, magnifier, and floss organizer)*

**DMC® Corporation,** South Kearney, New Jersey *(DMC® Coton Perle, Mouline Special 25 [6-strand cotton floss], DMC® tapestry needles)*

**gingher® INC.,** Greensboro, North Carolina *(scissors)*

**Kreinik Mfg., Inc.,** Baltimore, Maryland *(blending filaments)*

**Tomorrow's Treasures,** Woodinville, Washington *(floor stand, lap frame, scroll frames)*

**Zweigart®,** Somerset, New Jersey *(all the fabrics—Dublin, Belfast Linen, Cashel Linen, Hardanger, Lugana, Brittany, Aida #14, Aida #18)*

# Introduction

Counted-Thread techniques include Cross-Stitch, Assisi, Embroidery Stitches, Pattern Darning, Blackwork, Hardanger, and Pulled-Thread work. Each technique has been covered in a separate chapter with step-by-step instructions, clear diagrams, and photographs of each stitch and technique.

All Counted-Thread embroidery is worked by counting the fabric threads. Each stitch is worked over an exact specified number of vertical and horizontal threads (warp and weft). You must use evenweave fabric with the same number of threads per inch both horizontally and vertically.

There are chapters to introduce you to the latest tools and accessories, fabrics, threads and needles, vocabulary, preparation, and finishing.

This is a complete stitch reference guide for everyone who works or would like to learn to work Counted-Thread embroidery.

Always remember, this book is meant to be a learning guide for the novice and a reference book for the expert. It is *your* dictionary of Counted-Thread embroidery stitches from A to Z.

# THE NEW DICTIONARY OF
# COUNTED-THREAD
# EMBROIDERY STITCHES

# The Basics

## TOOLS AND ACCESSORIES

You do not need many complex tools to work Counted-Thread and other embroidery stitches on fabric. In fact, you can start with a piece of evenweave fabric, floss or other threads, a tapestry needle, and a pair of scissors. A frame, hoop, or scroll frame is usually used to keep the fabric taut.

### FABRICS

All charted or diagrammed stitches are worked on *evenweave* fabrics. This means that the fabric has the same number of threads to the inch in both the horizontal and vertical directions. These threads are called the warp (vertical) and the weft (horizontal). (See "Vocabulary," page 8.) I have used a selection of Zweigart® fabrics for the samples in this book, including Aida #14 and #18, Hardanger, Lugana, Dublin Linen, and Belfast Linen. (See "Fabrics," page 10.)

### FLOSS AND PERLE COTTON

All the samples in this book were worked with DMC® Cotton Floss and DMC® Perle Cotton #5, #8, #12, and #14. I chose DMC® for the quality of the products and the wide range of available colors.

The manufacturer advises that these threads can be hand- or machine-washed in a cool-temperature gentle cycle. I prefer to hand-wash my work. *Always check for colorfastness before washing.*

DMC® now has a new Rayon floss that works up beautifully with a high sheen. I suggest that you try it.

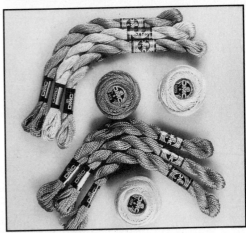

## FLOSS STORAGE

To avoid an unidentifiable tangle of threads, I recommend using one of the many storage items available for floss. These include plastic bags, organizers, and plastic or wood boxes.

The following two types have different approaches and advantages.

**The Color Caddy**™ is a dustproof plastic box with movable compartments that hold bobbins (plastic or cardboard) that are wound around with the whole skein of floss, uncut, in one long piece of thread. Each box holds approximately 125 full skeins of floss.

**The Lo-Ran® Thread Organizer** stores precut threads in a three-ring binder on punched cards for easy removal of threads. Each system will store 75 to 100 whole skeins of floss.

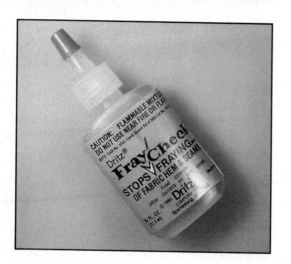

## FRAY CHECK®

This is a colorless plastic liquid that locks fabric or threads to prevent fraying. This product is an easy alternative to hemming or overcasting the edges of any fabric while working. It was used on many samples in this book.

## HOOPS

This is the most popular method for keeping a piece of fabric taut for working. A hoop set consists of two circles that fit together; sets are available in many sizes from 2″ to 36″. Hoops are made of wood, metal, and plastic in round and oval shapes.

*Note: Be careful to remove the fabric from the hoop when you are not working or a mark might be left on the fabric.*

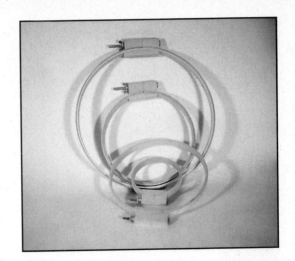

## MAGNETIC BOARD

This is a very useful aid for the stitcher who works with charts, diagrams, or written instructions. (Maybe that is why I always use one.) The Lo-Ran® board shown here is also made in 6″ × 10″ and 12″ × 18″. I recommend their accessory magnetic line magnifier for use with these boards. It really eases my eyestrain.

## MANUFACTURED NEEDLECRAFT PRODUCTS

Many soft-good items that can be used for Cross-Stitch, Pattern Darning, Assisi, and other forms of embroidery are readily available. I have used a few items from the Charles Craft line in this book (towels, napkins, and so forth). They are available at most craft and needlework stores.

## METALLIC THREADS

The Kreinik metallic threads used in this book are available in Blending Filament #4 and #8 Fine Braid, and #16 Medium Braid. They produce wonderful accent effects.

## NEEDLES

Counted Thread is worked with a blunt-tip tapestry needle, available in sizes #18, #20, #22, #24, and #26. The size of the needle you should use is determined by the thread count of the fabric. DMC® needles were used for the samples in this book.

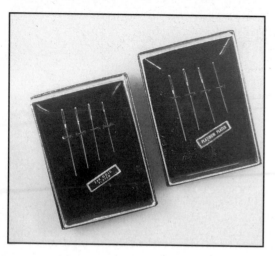

Kreinik Mfg., Inc. provided the 24K-gold-plated and platinum-plated needles shown here. They really make stitching extra smooth. Try them if you get the chance; it's fun to be a little extravagant.

## SCISSORS

I have always used and consider the **gingher®** INC. line of scissors to be the premier line of scissors available today.

The following are my favorite scissors for Counted-Thread work. A fine pair of scissors is a lifetime investment.

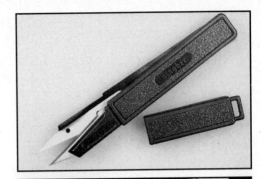

**4″ Thread Clip**

**31⁄2″ Embroidery Scissors**

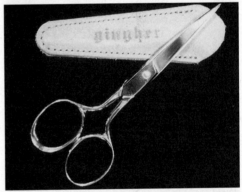

**4″ Embroidery Scissors**

## SCROLL FRAMES

Scroll frames keep the fabric taut and eliminate the possibility of hoop marks. The scroll rods, extender bars, and knobs as shown in the photograph can combine to make almost any size scroll frame.

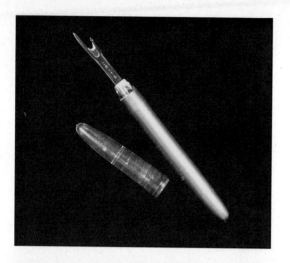

## SEAM AND STITCH RIPPER

This is a *must* tool for removing your mistakes quickly and safely.

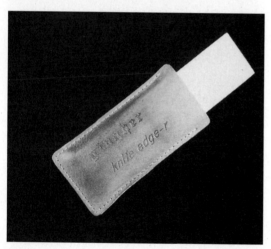

## SHARPENING STONE

This is a fine-grit whetstone used to sharpen and hone the blades of knife-edge scissors.

## STANDS

I have shown many different kinds of floor stands in my books, but this is the ultimate floor frame stand. It has every accessory and feature needed. Most of all, it is attractive and looks like a piece of fine furniture. I leave mine ready for work at all times. It is made by Tomorrow's Treasures. Look for it in needlework magazines and stores.

## STRETCHER STRIPS

This is the perfect alternative to the hoop or scroll frame. The fabric is attached to the frame with thumbtacks. No marks are left on the work in progress, but you must hem the edges of the fabric because it is often necessary to restretch the fabric to keep it taut.

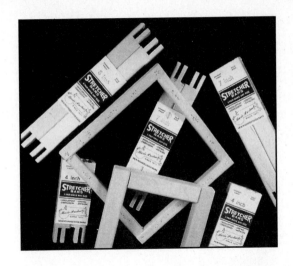

## TABLE STAND OR LAP FRAME

This is another Tomorrow's Treasures product and is also made like a piece of fine furniture. It adjusts to stay on the table or over your lap when you sit in a chair.

# VOCABULARY

**accent stitch** A surface stitch used for color or texture (usually by itself).

**Aida cloth** An evenweave fabric composed of four woven warp and weft threads.

**A.N.G.** American Needlework Guild.

**centimeter** A unit of measurement where 2.5 cm = 1″.

**compensation stitch** A partial stitch used to fill an area that is not large enough to hold a whole stitch.

**composite stitch** This is a stitch made up of two or more stitches.

**count** This is the number used to show the number of threads in an inch of fabric. In an evenweave fabric, it shows the number of threads in a square inch (horizontal and vertical threads).

**Counted Thread** An embroidery technique in which the stitches are worked over a *given*, specific number of fabric threads.

**drawn thread** Threads of the background fabric are cut and withdrawn.

**double darning** A form of Pattern Darning in which the fabric is totally covered with lines of running stitch.

**double-thread evenweave** Hardanger is an example of this fabric.

**E.G.A.** Embroiderers' Guild of America.

**evenweave** This is a type of fabric that has the identical thread count both horizontally and vertically.

**eye** The hole in the top of the needle that holds the thread.

**filling stitch** A stitch used to fill a predetermined shape on a ground fabric.

**floss** Six-stranded (6-ply) cotton embroidery thread.

**gauge** This is the count of horizontal and vertical threads in one square inch of fabric. If you have 14 threads it would be called #14 or 14-count fabric.

**Hardanger** A type of evenweave fabric that is woven with *pairs* of threads.

**hoop** An embroidery hoop is a type of frame consisting of two tightly fitted rings that are used to hold the fabric taut. It is also called a ring frame in many parts of the world.

**intersection** This is the point where the vertical and horizontal fabric threads cross.

**journey** A trip across the row. Some stitches may require two or more journeys to complete the stitch.

**Kloster Block** This is a group of Satin Stitches (usually five) used in Hardanger embroidery.

**laying tools** This is a stroking needle used to align the threads so that they will lay flat. You can use a needle trolley, Tekobari, or any large needle (such as a rug needle).

**motif stitch** This is a surface stitch that is usually worked alone as an accent stitch.

**needles** Needles come in many sizes with sharp or blunt tips. (See page 4.)

**needle threader** This is a small metal or plastic disk or rectangle with a hook or fine wire to catch the end of the thread.

**orts** These are the small pieces of thread (or yarn) that are trimmed from the starting and ending threads.

**ort bag** Used to collect your orts. Years ago, when thread was very expensive, these were saved to be used for stuffing.

**Perle Cotton (Coton Perle)** This is a type of twisted, shiny cotton embroidery thread. It is made in many weights and colors.

**plain weave** The most common type of fabric, where the vertical (warp) and horizontal (weft) threads are woven over and under each other singly.

**Pulled Thread** Some threads of the fabric are pulled together in a predetermined organized manner to create patterns with spaces or holes.

**right side** The side of the work meant to be seen.

**sampler** This is a sample of different embroidery stitches. It often contains an alphabet, the name of the stitcher, and the date. It is a learning project or practice piece. In American Colonial days, the sampler was used to teach numbers and letters to female children.

**scroll frame** An embroidery frame that consists of two rollers or bars placed between two upright pieces of wood or slats. The top and bottom of the fabric are attached to the rollers to hold the fabric taut.

**selvage** This is the woven or side edge of the fabric.

**single thread** Another name for evenweave fabric in which the vertical and horizontal fabric threads are single threads.

**splice** When you pierce or sew through the middle of a fabric thread.

**stranded cotton** This is another name for floss, a cotton embroidery thread made of 6 threads that can be used singly or in bundles of 2, 3, 4, 5, or 6.

**stretcher frame** A square or rectangular embroidery frame made of four wood bars or stretchers. The fabric is usually attached to the frame with rustproof thumbtacks.

**stripping** This is separating the 6 strands (or plys) into individual threads. They are then put back together in 2, 3, 4, 5, or 6 strands to achieve the desired weight of thread.

**tail** A piece of thread left at the end away from the needle and used to start the work. It should be no less than 3" to 4" long. The tail is woven into the back of the work at a later time.

**tapestry needle** A needle used for Counted-Thread work with a large eye and a blunt tip or point.

**warp** Vertical fabric threads.

**waste knot** This is the only acceptable knot used in needlework. It is used to hold the thread in place *temporarily* so that it can be covered with stitches or woven into the back of stitches (on the wrong side of the fabric).

**weft** Horizontal fabric threads.

**woof** This is the Old English word for *weft*.

**wrong side** This is the side of the fabric that is not seen. Most threads are started on the wrong side of the fabric.

# FABRICS

All fabrics used for the different kinds of Counted-Thread embroideries covered in this book are known as *evenweave fabrics*. They must have the same number of threads per inch in both the vertical (warp) and horizontal (weft) directions so that all the stitches will be squared and the same size.

They may be woven from a variety of natural fibers such as cotton, linen, or even wool. In recent times, synthetic and combination blends of natural and synthetic fibers have become popular because of the high cost of natural fibers and the added care necessary for their cleaning and maintenance. In my opinion, any embroidery that is meant to be passed down to future generations should be worked on the finest fabrics available.

Evenweave fabrics are measured and named by the number of threads per inch (or centimeter). For example, if the fabric measures 14 threads horizontally and 14 threads vertically it is called 14-count. *To determine* if a fabric is really an evenweave, work a basting line along one horizontal thread for 2" using a contrasting color sewing thread. Then work a vertical 2" line in the same manner, forming a right angle. Continue around to complete a 2" square. Count the vertical and horizontal fabric threads within the square. The fabric is evenweave if both counts are the same.

Most fabrics are manufactured in a wide variety of widths and colors. Fine linen is usually found only in white, off-white, or natural.

## SINGLE-THREAD EVENWEAVE

This is a plain weave of fabric in which each horizontal (weft) thread is woven over and under the vertical (warp) threads every time. It is woven in a wide variety of weights, from 14- to 36-count. This type of fabric is usually used for soft items such as clothing or household linens. Some linen fabrics have a loose weave, making them preferable for Pulled-Thread work.

## HARDANGER FABRIC

Hardanger fabric is woven as single-thread evenweave using pairs of threads to produce a double-threaded weave. The count for this fabric is 22 *pairs* of threads per inch. This is the traditional fabric used for Hardanger work, but it can be used for Cross-Stitch and many other Counted-Thread stitches. It is available in a wide variety of colors.

## AIDA CLOTH

This fabric is woven from multiples of 4 threads that produce a basketweave effect in each block of 4 threads with pronounced visible holes between each block. It is made in weights ranging from 6- to 18-count, making it suitable for Cross-Stitch, working each stitch over a single intersection of vertical and horizontal threads. Aida cloth is also available in a wide variety of colors.

# THREADS

Many different kinds of threads can be used for Counted-Thread embroidery. Some fibers are more suitable for each kind of work or technique.

The following threads and fibers are generally used for Counted-Thread work.

## FLOSS (STRANDED COTTON)

This is a silky textured thread made of 6 individual strands of cotton fiber. The strands can be separated into bundles of from 1 to 6 plies, depending upon the weight of the fabric and the effect desired.

This is the most popular and versatile thread used for embroidery and is available in hundreds of colors.

## PERLE COTTON (COTON PERLE)

This is made from 2 plies that are twisted to create what has been called a "pearl" effect. It is available in many thicknesses, from #3, the heaviest, to #12, the thinnest. Perle Cotton is used as a single strand, has a high luster, and is very strong. This is important when a stitch requires pulling the thread tightly. It can be used for many different Counted-Thread techniques.

## FLOWER THREAD

This is a soft textured cotton thread with a matte finish. It is available in many colors and may be used most successfully for Cross-Stitch.

## SILK AND RAYON THREADS

These fibers give a very luxurious look to any work and are available in stranded or twisted forms in many colors. Unfortunately they are difficult to work with and can be quite expensive. Through experience, I have found it worth the effort and expense.

## OTHER FIBERS

Metallic threads, crochet cottons, and linen and Rayon threads are also suitable for many Counted-Thread techniques. Don't be afraid to experiment.

# NEEDLES

## TAPESTRY NEEDLES

Most Counted-Thread techniques are worked with a large-eye, blunt-point tapestry needle. They are available in sizes from 13 (largest) to 26 (smallest). I recently saw a size 28 Danish needle included in a kit, but so far I haven't been able to locate the source.

## OTHER NEEDLES

*Sharps* are used for hand sewing and are considered to be all-purpose needles. *Darners* are used for basting because of their length. *Betweens* are smaller in length and easy to use. *Beading needles* are long, thin needles used for embellishing embroidery with beads. *Chenille* and *crewel* needles are large-eye, sharp-point needles used for surface stitching. None of these needles should be used for Counted-Thread work because the sharp points will split the fabric threads.

# MEASUREMENTS

A basic knowledge of measurements and conversions is used regularly by all needleworkers.

The question most often asked is how to determine the size of a design when a given pattern chart is to be worked on one size fabric instead of another.

The formula for making this determination is simple and requires very *basic* mathematics.

Always start by counting the number of squares on the chart (squares = stitches) in both the horizontal and vertical directions. Then count the number of vertical and horizontal threads in one square inch of your chosen fabric (if you don't already know the thread count of the fabric). Since all the works in this book are stitched on evenweave fabrics (see "Vocabulary," page 8), these numbers must be exactly the same.

The formula is *design area divided by threads per inch equals the size of the finished piece.* Therefore a 30 × 30 thread stitch design worked on #14 Aida would be 30 ÷ 14 = 2.1″.

This is the size of the finished *design* area. ALWAYS add 2″ to 3″ on all four sides of the fabric to provide a work border before you cut the fabric.

# The Stitch Dictionary A to Z

# A

## ASSISI EMBROIDERY

Assisi embroidery was originated in Italy in the town of Assisi sometime between the thirteenth and sixteenth centuries. It was first used by nuns to make ecclesiastical linens for their churches. The name Assisi embroidery wasn't applied to this technique until the twentieth century, when a revival occurred around the town of Assisi.

Assisi embroidery uses Cross-Stitches to make a background or negative image around unworked areas, forming motifs such as mythical or realistic animals, flowers, birds, or border designs of geometric patterns. Traditional church colors of dark red are used for the Cross-Stitch with black outlines on a light neutral-colored linen or evenweave fabric. The outlines are usually worked in the Holbein (Double Running) Stitch—however, Backstitch, Stemstitch, or even Chain Stitches can be tried. Details within the motifs are also worked in one of these outline stitches.

This type of embroidery is most often worked as an embellishment for clothing, household linens, or small accessories such as an eyeglass case, purse, or bookmark.

I prefer to work the outline in Perle Cotton and the Cross-Stitches in 6-strand embroidery floss. The number of plies (strands) of floss used will be determined by the thread count of the chosen fabric to provide even coverage.

### TO WORK

All stitches, Holbein and Cross-Stitch, are worked over the same number of fabric threads (2 horizontal and 2 vertical).

1. Work all the outlines.

2. Fill in the background with Cross-Stitches worked in horizontal lines. If you use a diagonal line in the outline, it will be necessary to use a half Cross-Stitch for compensation when you work the background near the diagonal outline. (See "Backstitch," page 94, "Holbein," page 129, and "Cross-Stitch," page 45.)

## ASSISI PATTERN #1 (MYTHICAL ANIMAL)

The sample is worked on Zweigart® Aida #14 with DMC® Cotton Floss (used 2-ply).

1. Mark center on fabric and diagram.

2. Work outline in Holbein or Backstitch using 2-ply Black Cotton Floss.

3. Fill in background in Cross-Stitch using 2-ply Red #666 Cotton Floss.

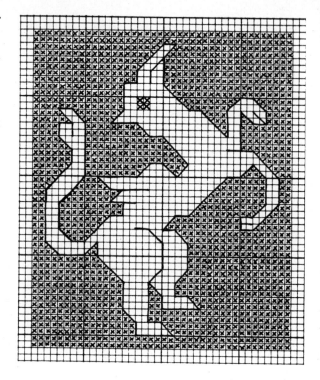

## ASSISI PATTERN #2
### (ELEPHANT WITH PICKET FENCE BORDER)

The sample is worked on Zweigart® Aida #14 with DMC® Cotton Floss (used 2-ply).

Instructions same as Pattern #1.

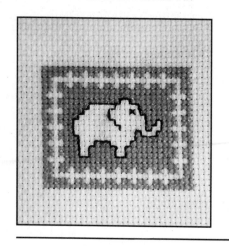

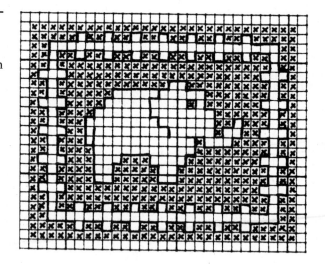

## ASSISI PATTERN #3 (ASSISI BIRD)

The sample is worked on Zweigart® Aida #14 with DMC® Cotton Floss (2-ply).

Instructions same as Pattern #1.

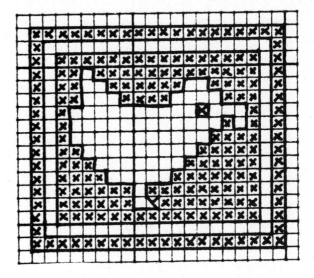

## ASSISI PATTERN #4

### (LEAVES WITH ROPE BORDER)

The sample is worked on Zweigart® Aida #14 with DMC® Cotton Floss (2-ply).

Instructions same as Pattern #1.

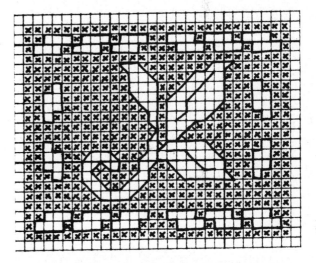

## ASSISI PATTERN #5 (SQUIRREL)

The sample is worked on Zweigart® Hardanger with DMC® Cotton Floss (used 2-ply for black and 3-ply for red).

Instructions same as Pattern #1.

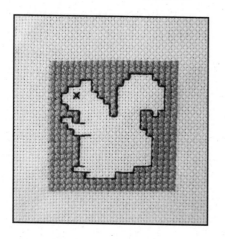

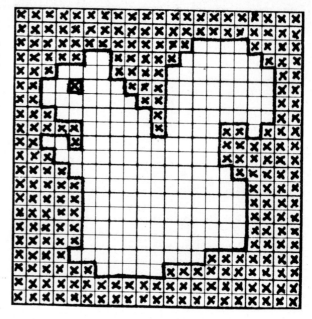

## BLACKWORK

Blackwork is a type of Counted-Thread embroidery that is thought to have originated in Spain because it shows a strong influence of the Moorish civilization that was dominant in Spain in the Middle Ages.

It was brought to England in the fourteenth century and was popularized by Catherine of Aragon (first wife of Henry VIII) in the sixteenth century.

Many examples of this embroidery can be found on portraits by Hans Holbein, a German painter at the English court. The Holbein Stitch, used in Blackwork embroidery (and also Assisi), was probably named for him.

Blackwork is usually worked on a white evenweave fabric with black thread—however, you will often see elaborate touches of gold and silver thread used to enhance the work. A softer effect will result from using brown thread on cream or beige fabric.

Blackwork is used to embellish clothing and household linens, or pictorially in wall hangings.

Single straight stitches are joined to form basic geometric patterns that are repeated to form the design. These include the Backstitch, Stem Stitch, Holbein Stitch (also called the Double Running Stitch), and Cross-Stitch. Most Cross-Stitchers find Blackwork very enjoyable because it uses a variety of stitch patterns.

Most evenweave fabrics are suitable for Blackwork embroidery. Linen was, and still is, the fabric of choice; however, many other evenweaves such as Aida or Hardanger work very well.

The weight of the thread used should be in proportion to the threads of the fabric. Six-strand floss and Perle Cotton are the most popular, but linen threads, some crochet cottons, and many metallic threads are also suitable for Blackwork.

Only blunt-tip tapestry needles are used for Blackwork. The size depends upon the fabric and thread used.

Blackwork should be worked on a frame to help hold the fabric taut. This will keep the fabric threads straight and easy to count. You can use a scroll frame or stretcher bars. (See "Tools and Accessories," page 1.) Many experts can work without a frame, but I think it is more difficult.

There are an infinite number of stitches charted and available for use in Blackwork. I always find it enjoyable to pick and choose the right one(s) for the project I am designing. You must be aware of the scale and density of the stitch and the size of the area to be filled. Dark areas require small stitch patterns while light areas require large, open patterns.

# BLACKWORK PATTERN #1 (BASIC BOX PATTERN)

The sample is worked on Zweigart® Aida #14 with DMC® #8 Perle Cotton.
   This is one of the patterns used as a base for many other Blackwork Patterns.

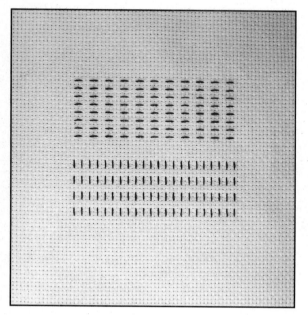 

**1.** Stitch a row of horizontal Running Stitches, working over and under 2 vertical fabric threads. See Diagram A.

**2.** The return trip is worked directly under the stitches of the previous row, leaving 2 unworked horizontal fabric threads between the rows.

**3.** Repeat these 2 rows until the desired area is filled.

**4.** Starting at 1, work vertical Running Stitches, being careful to avoid splitting the thread in the *shared* holes. See Diagram B.

**5.** After working this entire vertical row, come up from the back at 3 and continue in an upward direction. This will complete the first row of boxes.

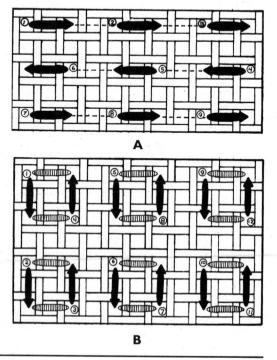

A

B

**6.** Diagram C shows an area filled with the box pattern.

*Note: This pattern can be worked over 2 or more fabric threads to create larger boxes.*

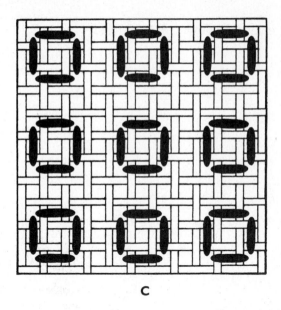

C

---

## BLACKWORK PATTERN #2

The sample is worked on Zweigart® Aida #18 with DMC® #12 Perle Cotton.

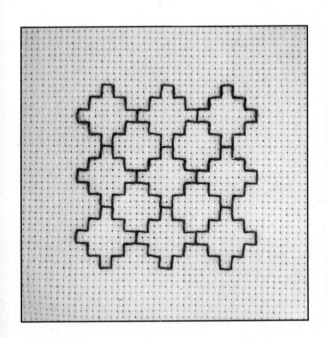

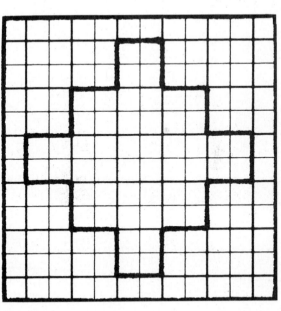

## BLACKWORK PATTERN #3

The sample is worked on Zweigart® Aida #18 with DMC® #12 Perle Cotton.

This is the same as Blackwork Pattern #2 with the addition of a Smyrna Stitch in the center.

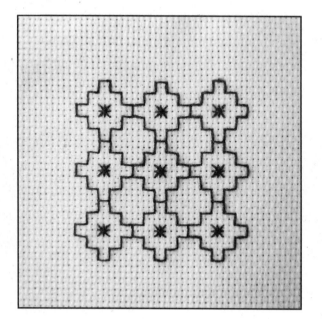 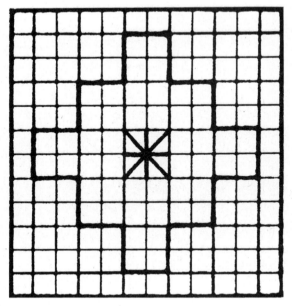

# BLACKWORK PATTERNS #4 AND #5

The sample is worked on Zweigart® Aida #18 with DMC® #12 Perle Cotton.

BLACKWORK PATTERN #4 AND #5

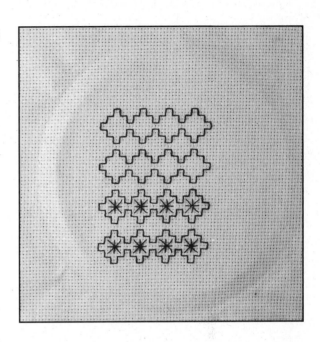

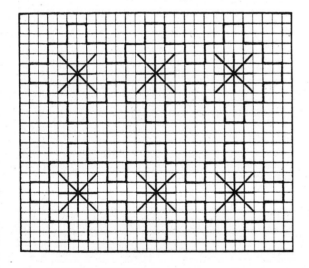

BLACKWORK PATTERN #5

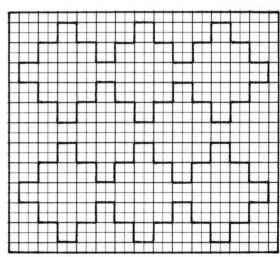

BLACKWORK PATTERN #4

# BLACKWORK PATTERNS #6 AND #7

The sample is worked on Zweigart® Aida #14 with DMC® #8 Perle Cotton.

Blackwork Pattern #7 is the same as Blackwork Pattern #6 with the addition of a Cross-Stitch in the center.

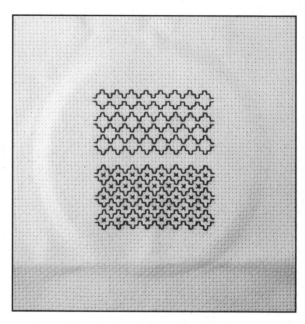

BLACKWORK PATTERNS #6 AND #7

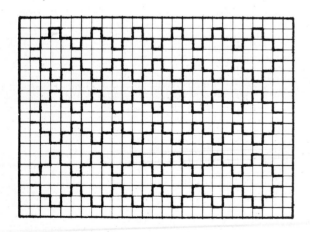

BLACKWORK PATTERN #6

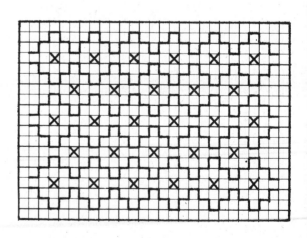

BLACKWORK PATTERN # 7

## BLACKWORK PATTERN #8

The sample is worked on Zweigart® Aida #14 with DMC® #8 Perle Cotton.

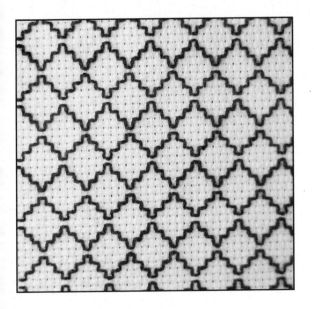
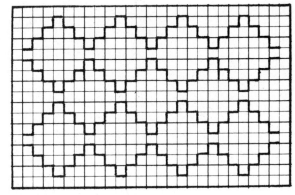

## BLACKWORK PATTERN #9

The sample is worked on Zweigart® Aida #14 with DMC® #8 Perle Cotton.

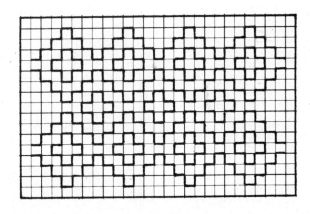

## BLACKWORK PATTERN #10

The sample is worked on Zweigart® Aida #14 with DMC® #8 Perle Cotton.

 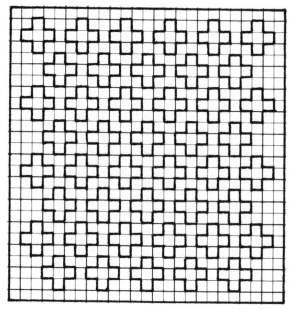

## BLACKWORK PATTERN #11

The sample is worked on Zweigart® Aida #14 with DMC® #8 Perle Cotton.

 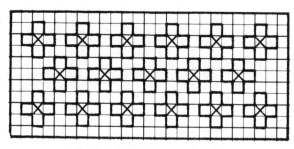

## BLACKWORK PATTERN #12

The sample is worked on Zweigart® Aida #14 with DMC® #8 Perle Cotton.

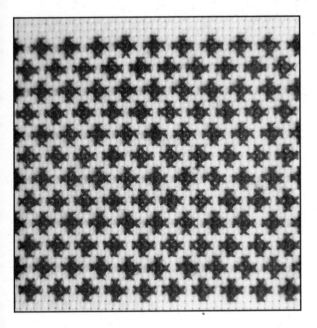
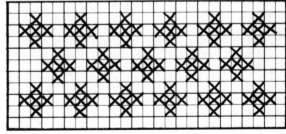

## BLACKWORK PATTERN #13

The sample is worked on Zweigart® Aida #18 with DMC® #12 Perle Cotton.

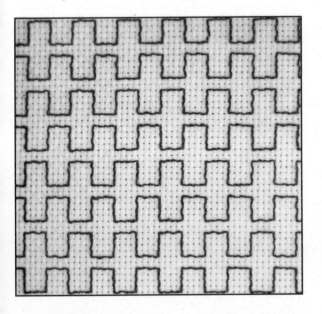
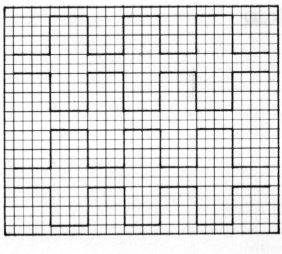

## BLACKWORK PATTERN #14

The sample is worked on Zweigart® Aida #18 with DMC® #12 Perle Cotton.

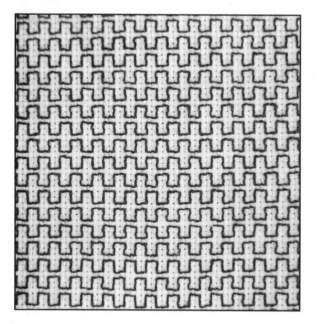 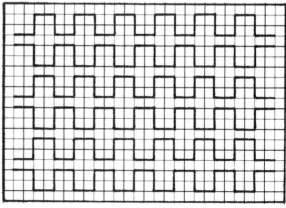

## BLACKWORK PATTERN #15

The sample is worked on Zweigart® Aida #18 with DMC® #12 Perle Cotton.

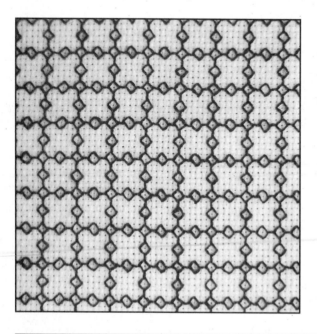 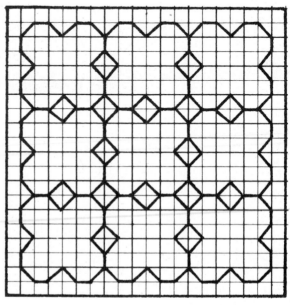

## BLACKWORK PATTERN #16

The sample is worked on Zweigart® Aida #18 with DMC® #12 Perle Cotton.

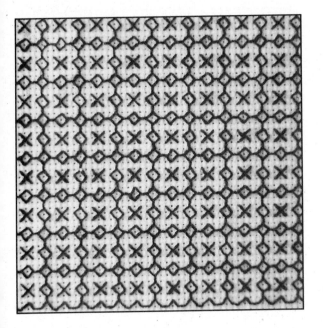

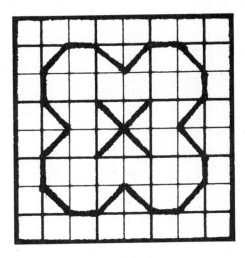

This is the same as Blackwork Pattern #15 with a Cross-Stitch in the center.

## BLACKWORK PATTERN #17

The sample is worked on Zweigart® Aida #18 with DMC® #12 Perle Cotton.

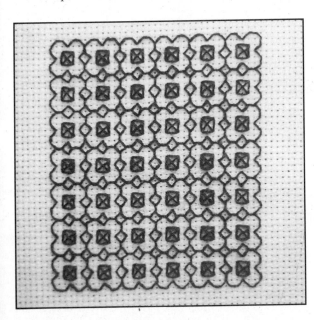

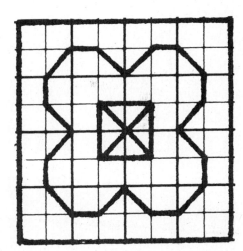

This is the same as Blackwork Pattern #15 with a Cross-Stitch in a square in the center.

## BLACKWORK PATTERN #18

The sample is worked on Zweigart® Aida #14 with DMC® #8 Perle Cotton.

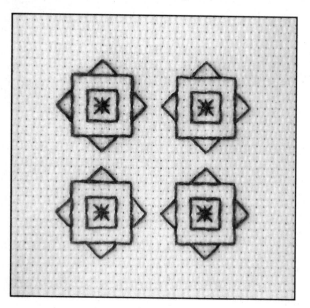 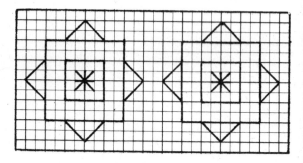

## BLACKWORK PATTERN #19

The sample is worked on Zweigart® Aida #14 with DMC® #8 Perle Cotton.

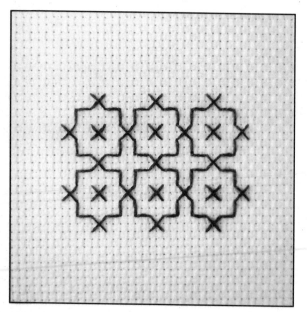 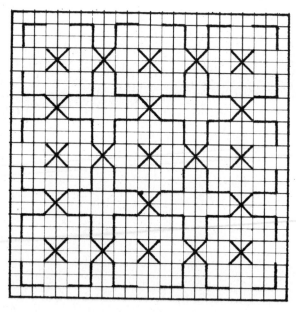

## BLACKWORK PATTERN #20

The sample is worked on Zweigart® Aida #14 with DMC® #8 Perle Cotton.
   This is a variation of Blackwork Pattern #19.

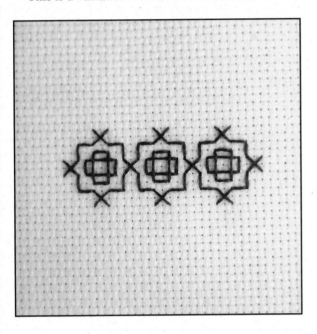
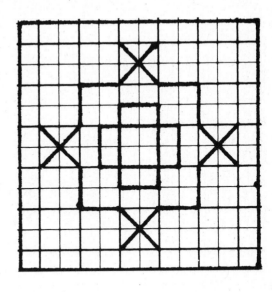

## BLACKWORK PATTERN #21

The sample is worked on Zweigart® Aida #14 with DMC® #8 Perle Cotton.
   This is another variation of Blackwork Pattern #19.

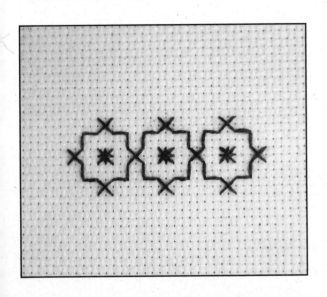
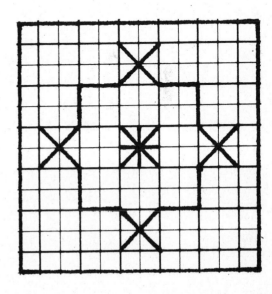

## BLACKWORK PATTERN #22

The sample is worked on Zweigart® Aida #14 with DMC® Cotton Floss.

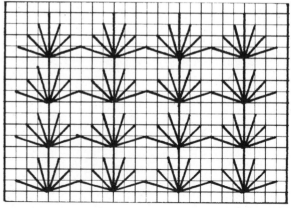

## BLACKWORK PATTERN #23

The sample is worked on Zweigart® Aida #18 with DMC® Cotton Floss.

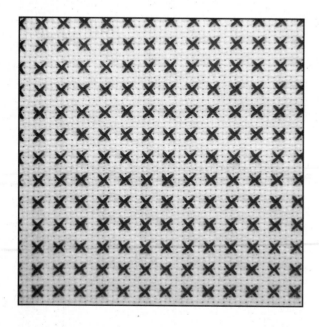

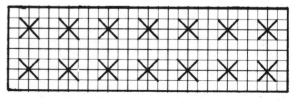

Blackwork Patterns #23, #24, #25, and #26 show the progression of a stitch. Each pattern changes with the addition of 1 or 2 lines.

## BLACKWORK PATTERN #24

The sample is worked on Zweigart® Aida #18 with DMC® Cotton Floss.

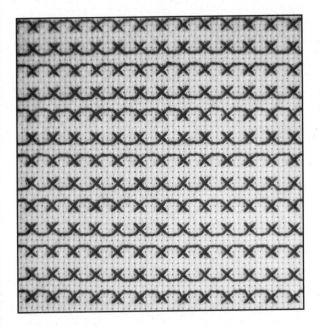
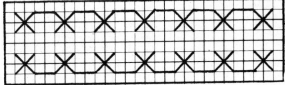

## BLACKWORK PATTERN #25

The sample is worked on Zweigart® Aida #18 with DMC® Cotton Floss.

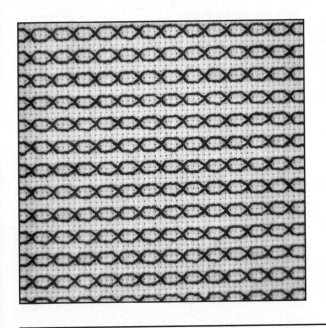
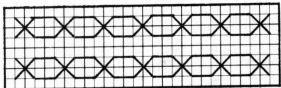

## BLACKWORK PATTERN #26

The sample is worked on Zweigart® Aida #18 with DMC® Cotton Floss.

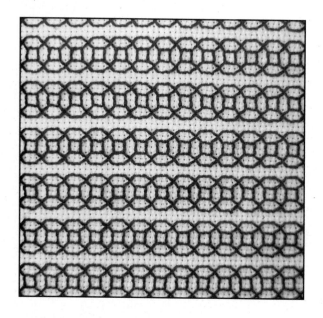 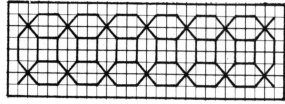

## BLACKWORK PATTERN #27

The sample is worked on Zweigart® Aida #14 with DMC® Cotton Floss.
   This can be used as a border pattern.

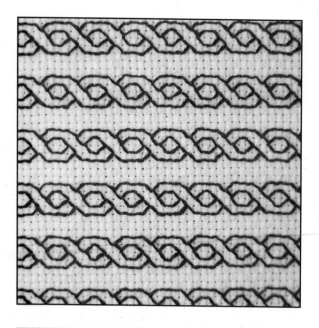 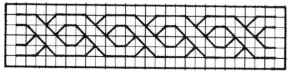

## BLACKWORK PATTERN #28

The sample is worked on Zweigart® Aida #18 with DMC® Cotton Floss.

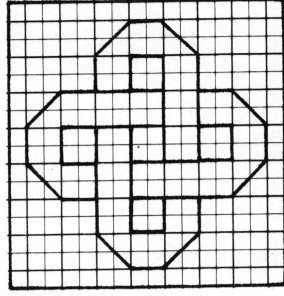

## BLACKWORK PATTERN #29

The sample is worked on Zweigart® Aida #18 with DMC® Cotton Floss.

33

## BLACKWORK PATTERN #30

The sample is worked on Zweigart® Aida #18 with DMC® Cotton Floss.

## BLACKWORK PATTERN #31

The sample is worked on Zweigart® Aida #18 with DMC® Cotton Floss.

## BLACKWORK PATTERN #32

The sample is worked on Zweigart® Aida #14 with DMC® Perle Cotton.
This pattern uses the Holbein Stitch. (See page 129.)

 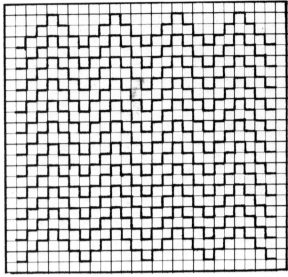

## BLACKWORK PATTERN #33

The sample is worked on Zweigart® Aida #14 with DMC® #8 Perle Cotton.
This pattern is worked using the Holbein Stitch. (See page 129.)

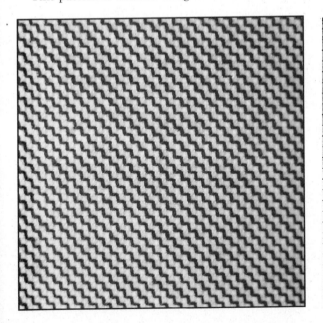 

## BLACKWORK PATTERN #34

The sample is worked on Zweigart® Aida #18 with DMC® #12 Perle Cotton.

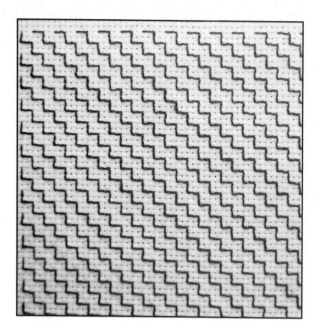 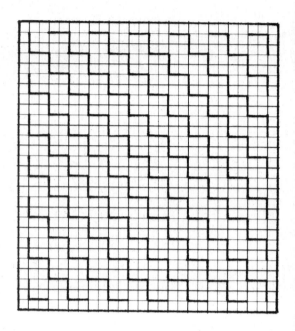

## BLACKWORK PATTERN #35

The sample is worked on Zweigart® Aida #18 with DMC® #12 Perle Cotton.

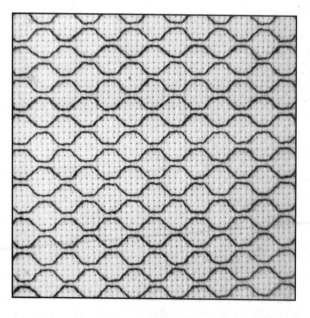 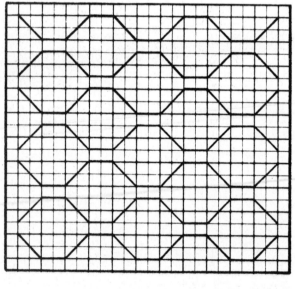

## BLACKWORK PATTERN #36

The sample is worked on Zweigart® Aida #18 with DMC® #12 Perle Cotton and DMC® Cotton Floss (1-ply) for the Cross-Stitches.

    This is the same as Blackwork Pattern #35 with the addition of the Cross-Stitch.

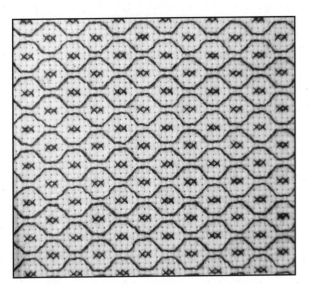 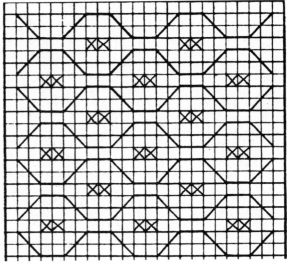

## BLACKWORK PATTERN #37

The sample is worked on Zweigart® Aida #18 with DMC® #12 Perle Cotton.

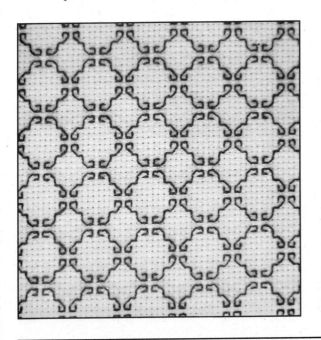 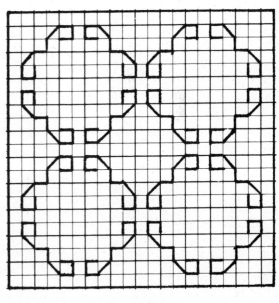

## BLACKWORK PATTERN #38

The sample is worked on Zweigart® Aida #18 with DMC® #12 Perle Cotton.

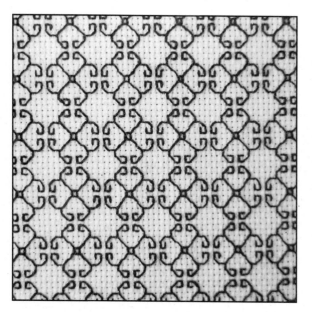 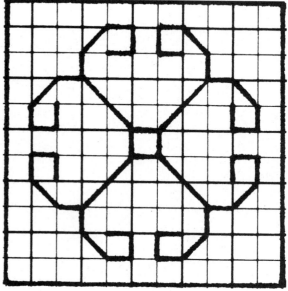

## BLACKWORK PATTERN #39

The sample is worked on Zweigart® Aida #18 with DMC® #12 Perle Cotton.

 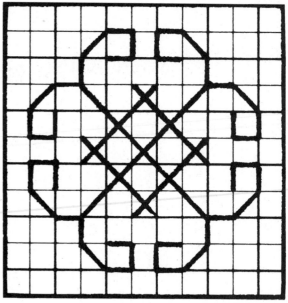

## BLACKWORK PATTERN #40

The sample is worked on Zweigart® Aida #18 with DMC® #12 Perle Cotton and DMC® Cotton Floss (1- or 2-ply) for Cross-Stitches.

 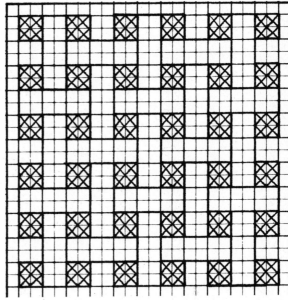

## BLACKWORK PATTERN #41

The sample is worked on Zweigart® Aida #18 with DMC® #8 Perle Cotton.

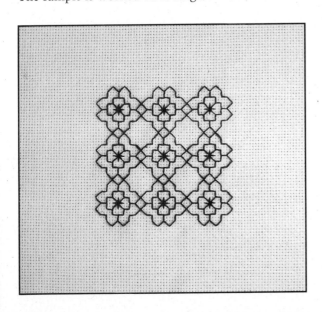 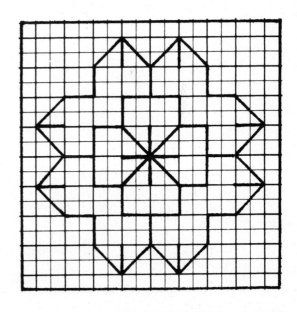

## BLACKWORK CORNER #1

The sample is worked on Zweigart® Aida #18 with DMC® Cotton Floss.
   This works up as a beautiful rope pattern border.

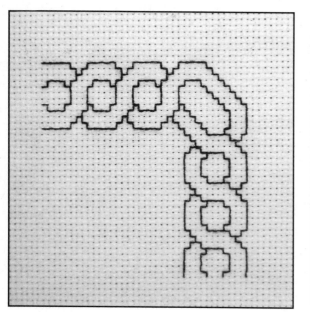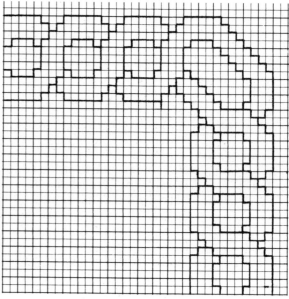

## BLACKWORK CORNER #2

The sample is worked on Zweigart® Aida #18 with DMC® Cotton Floss.

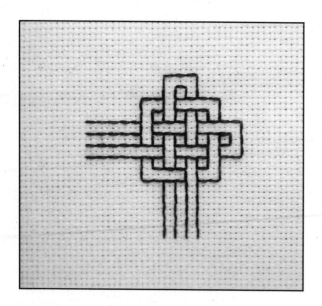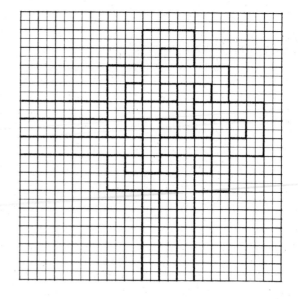

## BLACKWORK CORNER #3

The sample is worked on Zweigart® Lugana with DMC® Cotton Floss.

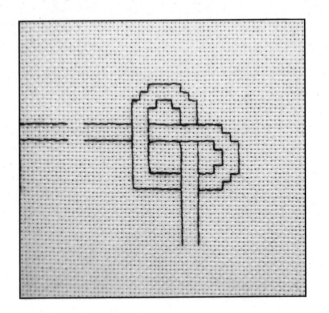
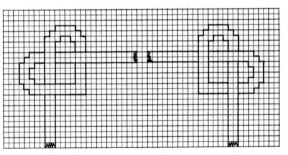

# E

# EMBROIDERY STITCHES

Counted-Thread embroidery is worked by counting fabric threads to create the stitches. Each stitch is made by working over a predetermined number of fabric threads in a numbered sequence. You *must* use evenweave fabric.

*Note: Many needlepoint stitches can be adapted for Counted-Thread embroidery on evenweave fabric. Experiment—you will be pleasantly surprised. (See the book* The New Dictionary of Needlepoint & Canvas Stitches *by Rhoda Goldberg for diagrams of many of these stitches.)*

## ALGERIAN EYE

The sample is worked on Zweigart® Aida #18 with DMC® Cotton Floss #604.

The Algerian Eye Stitch works as a border, frame, or allover Counted-Thread filling stitch. It is worked with almost no pull as a surface embroidery stitch. When used for Pulled-Thread embroidery, use a firm pull.

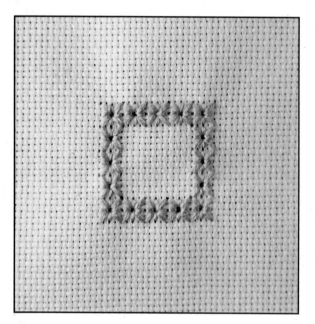

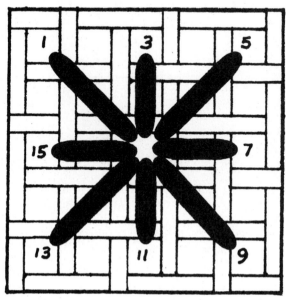

This is a very simple stitch that is worked following the diagram numbers exactly as shown.

## CRETAN STITCH

The sample is worked on Zweigart® Hardanger with DMC® Cotton Floss #604 (used 6-ply).

This stitch is usually used as a border, alone, or in combination with other Counted-Thread stitches (for example, Satin Stitch). It can be worked over varying numbers of fabric threads that will form a more open or closed pattern.

*Note: The second sample row was worked in 3-ply floss with a shorter stitch (over 2 fabric threads) to show an example of a possible variation.*

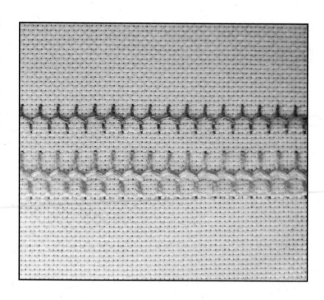

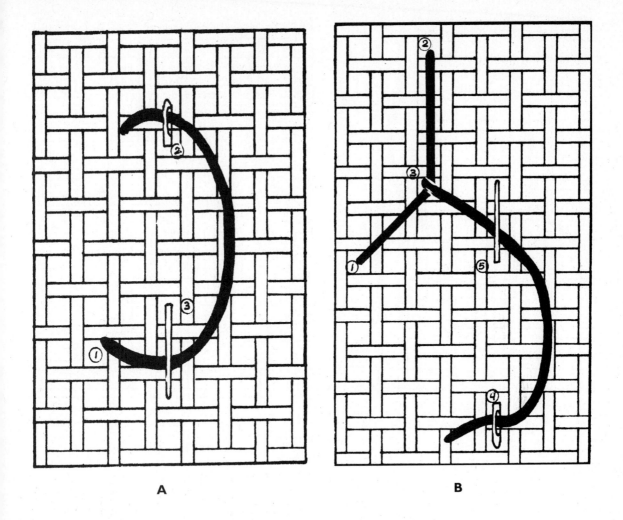

A              B

**1.** As shown in Diagram A, bring the thread up from the back at 1 and put it down at 2 (6 fabric threads up and 2 fabric threads to the right). Bring the needle to the front at 3 (4 fabric threads down) with the needle placed over the thread.

**2.** Put the needle down at 4 (6 fabric threads down and 2 fabric threads to the right), bringing the needle to the front at 5 (Diagram B). Again, remember to keep the needle over the thread.

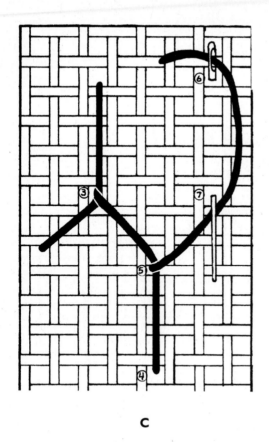

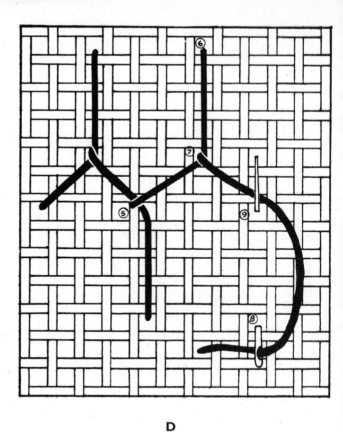

C

D

**3.** As shown in Diagram C, put the needle down at 6 (6 fabric threads up and 2 to the right), bringing it to the front at 7 (4 fabric threads down). Again, remember to keep the needle over the thread.

**4.** As shown in Diagram D, put the needle down at 8 (6 fabric threads down and 2 fabric threads to the right), bringing it to the front at 9 (4 fabric threads up). Again, remember to keep the needle over the thread. Continue working this way across the row.

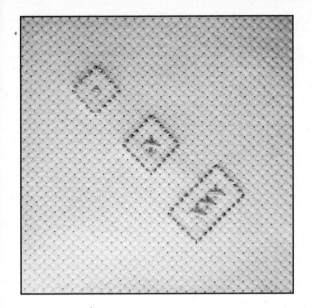

## CROSS-STITCH

The sample is worked on Zweigart® Aida #14 with DMC® Cotton Floss.

This is the first Counted-Thread embroidery stitch learned by most stitchers. It is still the most popular and well-known introductory stitch used today.

**1.** Bring the thread up from the back at 1 and down at 2, up at 3 and down at 4. This will complete 1 unit of Cross-Stitch over the intersection of 1 vertical and 1 horizontal fabric thread.

**2.** When Cross-Stitch is worked on linen (or linen-type blends), always work over 2 horizontal and 2 vertical fabric threads.

*Note: This diagram shows a group of Cross-Stitches worked in a row. Follow the numbering sequence.*

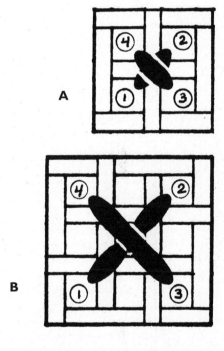

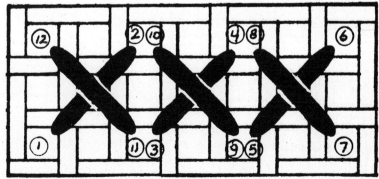

## DOUBLE LEVIATHAN

The sample is worked on Fiddlers Cloth with DMC® Cotton Floss #604.

This Counted-Thread stitch can be used as a border as shown in the sample or as a decorative accent stitch.

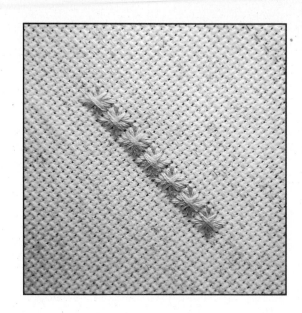

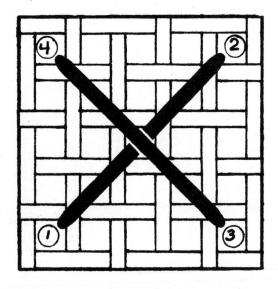

**A**

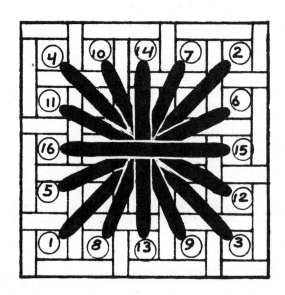

**B**

Follow the numbering as shown on the diagrams *exactly* or you will not create the textured bump on the surface of the stitch.

# FERN

The sample is worked on Zweigart® Aida #14 with DMC® Cotton Floss #905 (used 4-ply).

This is a Counted-Thread stitch worked in a woven braid in *vertical* rows. You can use it as a border or filler stitch in single or multiple rows. It is often used to represent feathers or foliage.

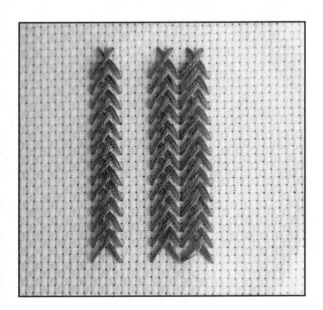 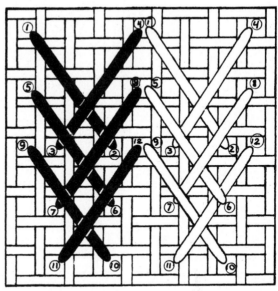

1. Come up from the back at 1 and down over 4 horizontal and 3 vertical fabric threads at 2.

2. Come up under 2 vertical fabric threads at 3 and down over 4 horizontal and 3 vertical fabric threads at 4.

3. Each unit is started 2 horizontal fabric threads below the first stitch of the last unit.

# HERRINGBONE (PLAITED GOBELIN)

The sample is worked on Fiddlers Cloth with DMC® Cotton Floss Ecru and #604.

This is a woven linear stitch that is *always* worked from left to right in horizontal rows. The sample shows 4 rows worked in 2 colors as a wide border and as a single border row.

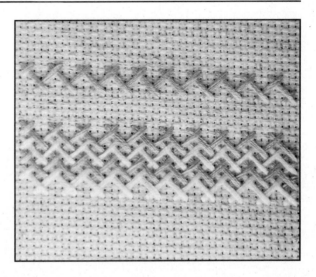

**1.** Come up from the back at 1 and down over 2 horizontal and 2 vertical fabric threads at 2.

**2.** Come up at 3 (under 2 vertical fabric threads) and down over 4 horizontal and 4 vertical fabric threads at 4.

**3.** Come up at 5 (under 2 vertical fabric threads) and down at 6 (over 4 horizontal and 4 vertical fabric threads). Continue in this way across the row.

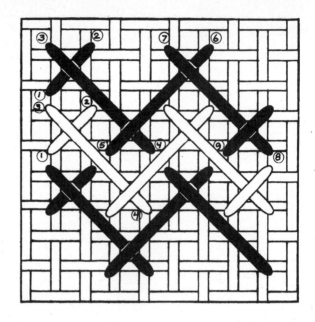

## INTERWOVEN CROSS
### (INTERLACED CROSS, WOVEN CROSS)

The sample is worked on Zweigart® Aida #14 with DMC® Cotton Floss.

The Interwoven Cross is a square stitch that is used as a single accent stitch or worked in rows to form a border or filling. This stitch is worked over 4 horizontal and 4 vertical fabric threads.

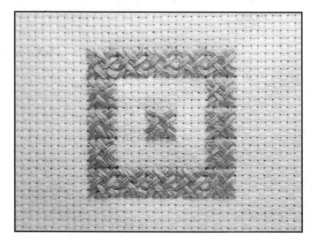

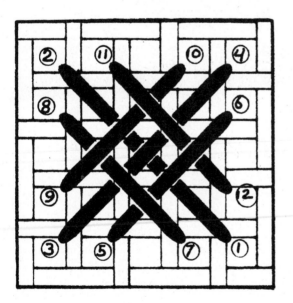

**1.** Following the numbers on the diagram, make a basic Cross-Stitch (see page 45) over 4 horizontal and 4 vertical fabric threads.

**2.** Next, come up at 5 and down at 6, up at 7 and down at 8, up at 9 and down at 10.

**3.** For the last stitch, come up at 11, over 3–4 and 9–10, and slip the needle *under* the last stitch (5–6), going down at 12. This maintains the pattern.

## LEAF

The sample is worked on Zweigart® Hardanger with DMC® Cotton Floss #905 (used 4-ply).

The Leaf Stitch is one of the most widely used ornamental stitches. It can be worked as shown on the sample as a single motif (used 6-ply) or grouped in horizontal rows as a border or filling stitch (4-ply was used in the sample for the multiple rows).

1. Bring the needle up from the back at 1 and down at 2 (over 4 horizontal and 3 vertical fabric threads). Continue in this way for 3–4 and 5–6.

2. Bring the needle to the front at 7 (5 horizontal and 2 vertical fabric threads to the right) and down at 8.

3. Return to the front at 9 (under 5 horizontal fabric threads up and 1 vertical fabric thread to the right) and down at 10.

4. Bring the needle up to the front at 11 (under 5 horizontal fabric threads up) and down at 12 (over 3 horizontal fabric threads down).

5. Continue in this way following the numbers on the diagram exactly.

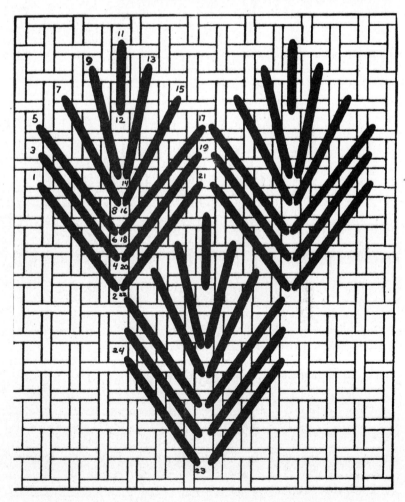

## LONG-ARMED CROSS (DOUBLE BACK CROSS, GREEK CROSS, LONG-LEGGED CROSS)

The sample is worked on Zweigart® Aida #14 with DMC® Cotton Floss (used 6-ply).

The Long-Armed Cross is worked in horizontal rows that resemble an interwoven braid. It can be used as a single-row border, or in multiple rows to create a wide border, or even as filling.

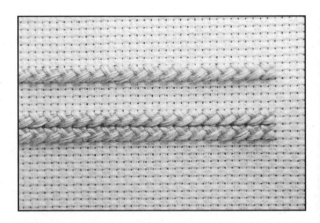

**1.** Begin with a Cross-Stitch worked over 2 horizontal and 2 vertical fabric threads (1–2, 3–4).

**2.** Come back to the front in the same hole as the first stitch and go over 2 horizontal and 4 vertical fabric threads, making the long arm (5–6).

**3.** Go under 2 horizontal fabric threads, coming up at 7, and go down at 8 (over 2 horizontal and 2 vertical fabric threads).

**4.** Continue from the long arm at (9) across the row as shown in the diagram.

*Note: For the sample I have shown a single row and a double row. Both were worked from left to right. If you turn the fabric for the second row, a different pattern will be created.*

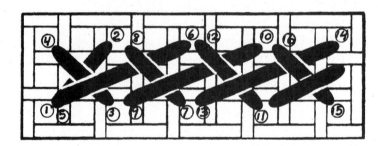

## RHODES STITCH

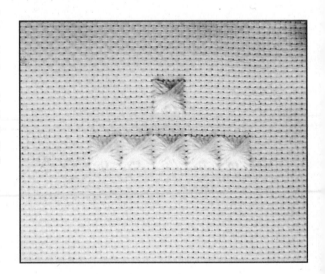

The sample is worked on Zweigart® Hardanger with DMC® Cotton Floss #800 (used 4-ply) and Ecru (used 2-ply).

This stitch was created by the British designer and author Mary Rhodes. It can be worked over an area of from 3 to 24 or more fabric threads and is used as an individual decorative motif, a border, or even a filling. *Always remember that this is a very heavy square stitch with a large amount of texture.*

Following the numbers on the diagram exactly, working from 1–2 (3–4, etc.) in a counterclockwise direction.

## SATIN STITCH

The sample is worked on 18-count Zweigart® Aida with DMC® Cotton Floss.

The Satin Stitch can be worked vertically (Diagram C), horizontally (variation 1), diagonally (variation 2), or in a shape over varying numbers of threads (variation 3).

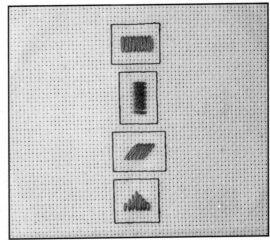

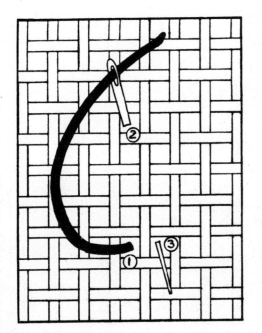

### SATIN STITCH (VERTICAL)

1. As shown in Diagram A, bring the thread through to the front at 1. Bring it down at 2 (4 horizontal threads up) and bring it out at 3 (4 horizontal threads down and 1 vertical thread to the right).

**A**

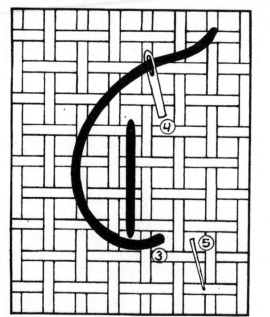

**B**

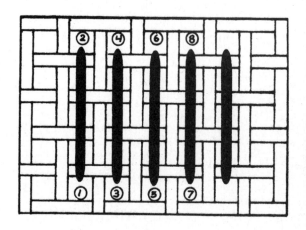

**C**

**2.** As shown in Diagram B, next, insert the needle at 4 (4 horizontal threads up) and bring it to the front at 5 (4 horizontal threads down and 1 vertical thread to the right).

**3.** Continue working the stitches in this manner (Diagram C).

## SATIN STITCH (HORIZONTAL), VARIATION I.

This diagram shows the Satin Stitch worked on the horizontal.

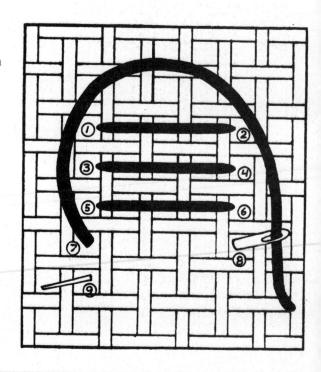

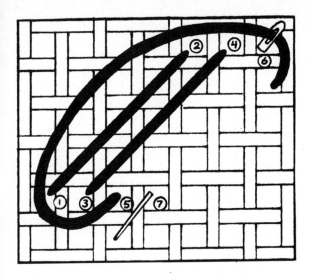

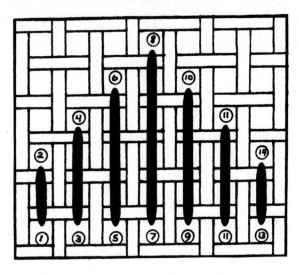

## SATIN STITCH (DIAGONAL), VARIATION 2.

This diagram shows the Satin Stitch worked on the diagonal.

## SATIN STITCH (SHAPE), VARIATION 3.

This diagram shows the Satin Stitch worked vertically over varying numbers of fabric threads.

The photograph on page 51 shows all four Satin stitches.

## SMYRNA CROSS (DOUBLE CROSS, LEVIATHAN)

The sample is worked on Zweigart® Hardanger with DMC® Cotton Floss.

This stitch can be worked over any even number of horizontal and vertical fabric threads (2, 4, 6, 8, etc.).

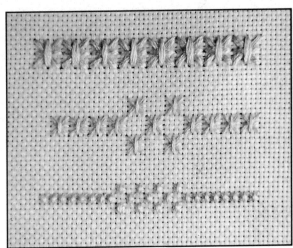

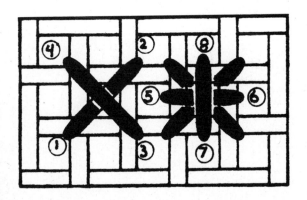

Follow the numbering on the diagram. It will be the same sequence of numbers over any even number of fabric threads.

## HARDANGER

Hardanger is a method of openwork embroidery that originated in Norway. It spread to the other Scandinavian countries, all over Europe, and was finally brought to the United States by immigrants from the Scandinavian countries.

Hardanger embroidery *must* be worked on an evenweave fabric. Today, it is generally worked on Hardanger cloth (a #22 evenweave cotton, woven with pairs of threads), available in the traditional white or ivory and in a very large variety of colors. It can be worked on other evenweave fabrics.

Perle Cotton is the thread used in Hardanger work. For the Kloster Blocks (Satin Stitches, Buttonhole Edging, and individual motifs) use a thread that is a little heavier than the threads of the fabric. Most people use Perle Cotton #5 on #22 Hardanger cloth. Use #8 or #12 Perle Cotton for the finer work of covering the bars and working the filling stitches. Two strands of embroidery floss may be substituted for #12 Perle Cotton if you cannot obtain #12 in your chosen color.

Hardanger is always worked with tapestry needles. Your scissors must have very sharp points to achieve a neat appearance in the cutwork.

Although Hardanger can be worked in the hand by experts, I suggest you work with a frame or hoop. Your stitches will have a neat, more even appearance and it will be easier to count the fabric threads.

Satin Stitch motifs (see page 51) and eyelets are used to fill and embellish open areas of fabric.

## BUTTONHOLE EDGING

The sample is worked on Zweigart® Hardanger with #5 Perle Cotton.

This is a traditional edge finish for Hardanger embroidery. It can be worked alone or around Satin Stitch Kloster Blocks. Each stitch covers 4 fabric threads (horizontal or vertical).

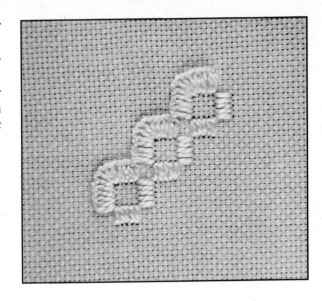

**1.** First work the Kloster Blocks (see page 57).

**2.** To start the Buttonhole edge, come up at 1 and down at 2, returning to the front at 1. Come down at 3 and up at 4 pulling the needle and thread through a loop formed by the thread. Diagram A shows 4 Buttonhole Stitches worked this way.

*Note: A ridge is formed at the top of these stitches by pulling the thread through the loop.*

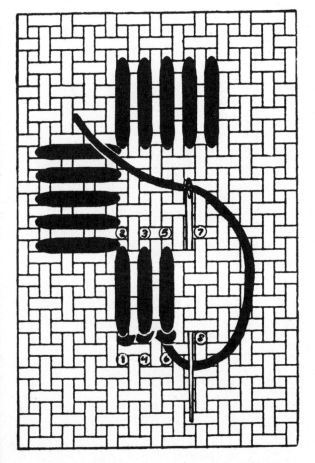

**A**

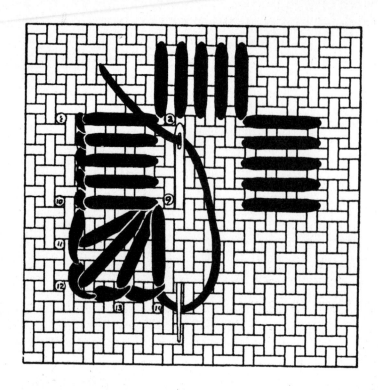

3. Complete 5 Buttonhole Stitches to correspond with the 5 Satin Stitch Kloster Block. Then, to turn a smooth corner, work 3 diagonal Buttonhole Stitches from the corner hole of the fifth Satin Stitch (9–11, 9–12, 9–13).

4. The neat stitch (9–14) becomes the first stitch of the next Kloster Block.

*Note: 5 stitches share the corner hole.*

5. When the Buttonhole edge is complete, trim the fabric as close to the ridge edge as you can without cutting the thread.

B

## HEDEBO BUTTONHOLE EDGING

The sample is worked on Zweigart® Hardanger with DMC® #8 Perle Cotton.
   Hedebo Buttonhole edging forms a larger ridge than Buttonhole edging and is worked on the folded edge of the fabric.

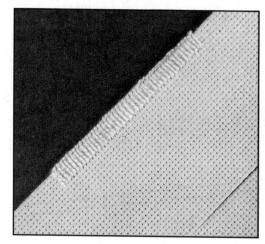

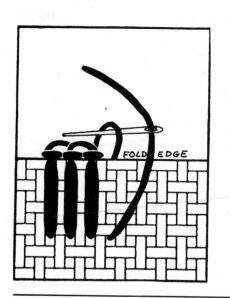

1. Fold the fabric to make the edge.

2. Bring the needle up at the left edge of the fold.

3. Bring the needle to the front (4 horizontal fabric threads down) and put the needle through the loop formed (from right to left).

4. Continue across in this way.

## KLOSTER BLOCKS (SATIN STITCH)

The sample is worked on Zweigart® with DMC® #5 Perle Cotton.

This is the basic stitch block or foundation stitch of Hardanger embroidery. The blocks consist of 5 straight Satin Stitches worked over 4 fabric threads and are called Kloster Blocks.

*Note:* Never have a diagonal *stitch on the back. All stitches must be horizontal or vertical.*

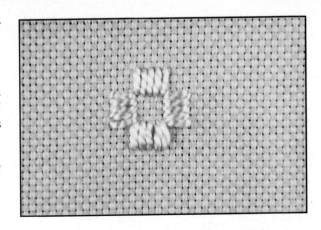

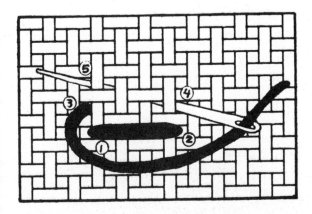

1. Bring the needle to the front at 1. Put it down at 2 (over 4 vertical fabric threads to the right) and back up to the front at 3 (under 4 vertical fabric threads and up 1 horizontal thread). Return to the back at 4 and up at 5.

**A**

2. Continue in this way until 4 Satin Stitches are completed. To complete the block and turn the corner to start a second block over the horizontal fabric threads, insert the needle at 10 and bring it back up to the front at 11 (under 4 horizontal fabric threads).

**B**

C

D

**3.** Return to hole 10 and come up under 4 horizontal and 1 vertical fabric threads. Complete the block of 5 Satin Stitches.

**4.** This diagram shows another way to start a corner. Repeat from step 1 for a third block using hole 18 to start.

## HARDANGER CUTTING

The samples are worked on Zweigart® Hardanger with DMC® #5 Perle Cotton.

*Note:* Never *cut a fabric thread that is parallel to a Satin Stitch. Always cut across the ends of the Satin Stitch.*

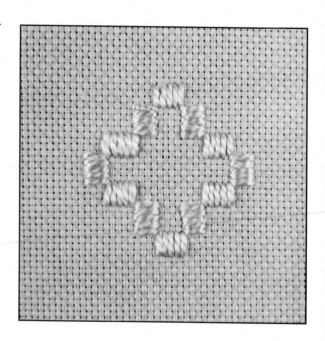

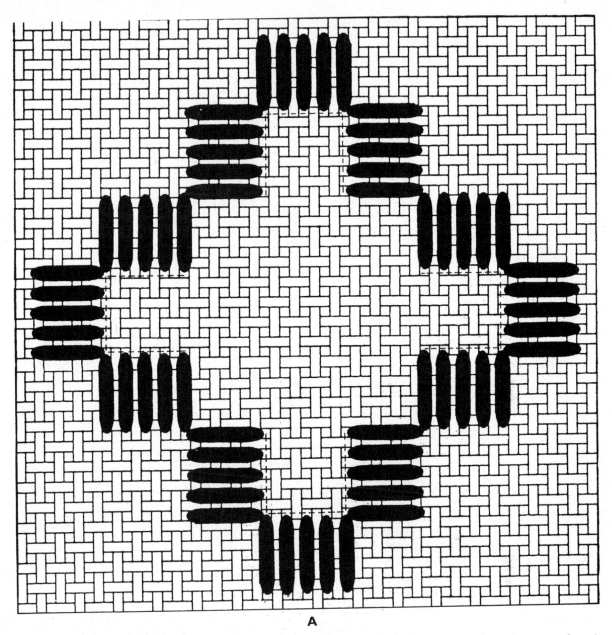

A

**1.** Keep the Satin Stitches to the right of the scissor blades (to the left if you are left-handed). Insert the scissor blade tip into the end hole and cut across 4 fabric threads. Snip as close to the Satin Stitches as you can without cutting the Perle Cotton. Continue cutting around as indicated on the diagram.

**2.** Pull out all loose fabric threads, leaving the threads to be wrapped as shown on the diagram.

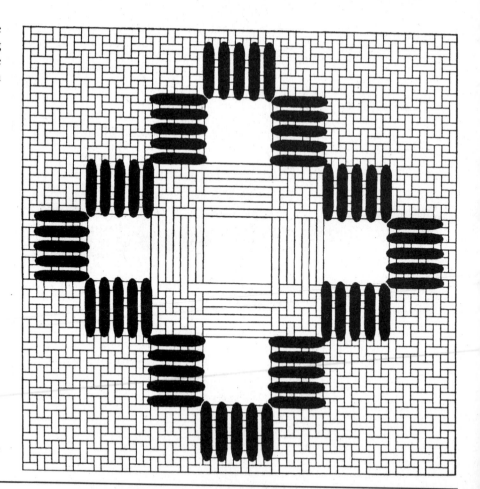

B

## HARDANGER WRAPPING
### (OVERCAST BARS OVER ALL THREADS)

The sample is worked on Zweigart® Hardanger with DMC® #5 and #8 Perle Cotton.

When you complete the cutting, groups of 4 fabric threads will be left. In this procedure they will be wrapped into *bars*.

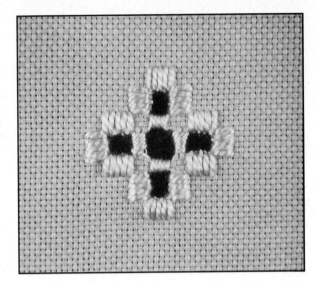

**1.** Secure the thread in the back of a block of Satin Stitches.

**2.** Bring the needle to the front and wrap the thread around all 4 fabric threads.

**3.** Continue wrapping around these threads to the end of the bar.

**4.** Carry the thread across the back to the next group of 4 fabric threads and continue wrapping in the same way.

**5.** Repeat for the rest of the fabric threads to be wrapped into bars unless you are planning to work a filling stitch. To work a filling stitch, 1 side may have to be left unworked.

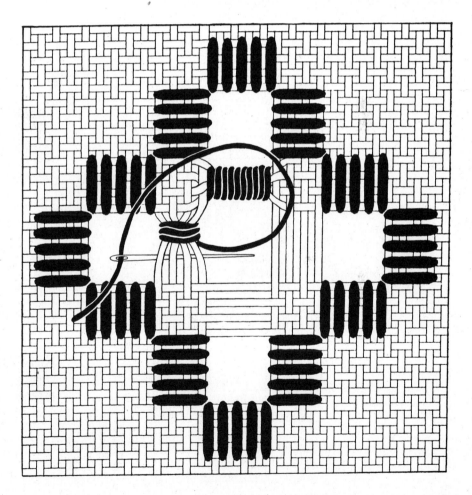

# HARDANGER WRAPPING
## (OVERCAST BARS OVER HALF THREADS)

The sample is worked on Zweigart® Hardanger with DMC® #5 and #8 Perle Cotton.

This procedure forms 2 bars from each of the groups of 4 threads to be wrapped. It is worked exactly as Overcast Bars over all threads (see page 61).

Follow the diagram below for the direction of the wrapping.

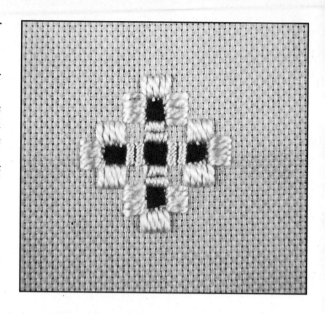

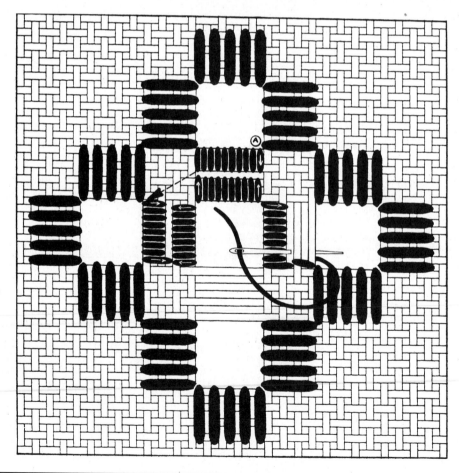

# HARDANGER WEAVING (WOVEN BARS)

In this procedure, the 4 fabric threads remaining after cutting are woven into bars.

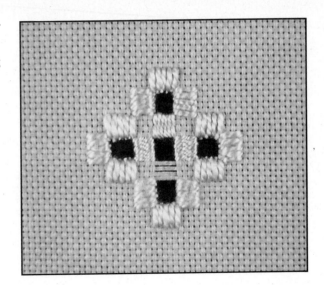

**1.** Weave the starting thread in the back into a group of Satin Stitches. Bring the needle to the front of the fabric in the middle of the 4 threads.

**2.** Bring the needle around the 2 threads on 1 side and back to the middle.

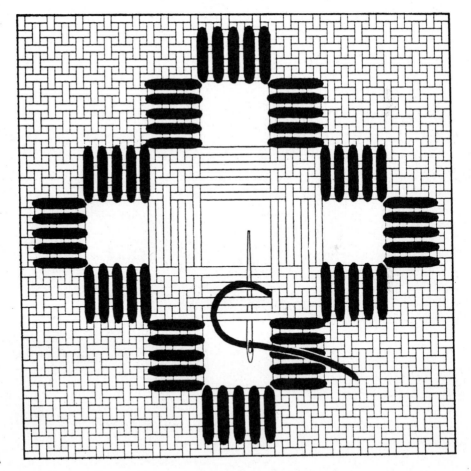

A

**3.** Repeat on the 2 threads of the opposite side.

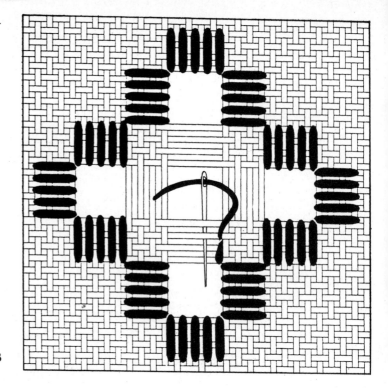

B

**4.** Continue weaving in this figure eight pattern to the end of the bar. *The weaving must be very firm and even.*

**5.** After 1 bar is complete, cross over to the next group of 4 fabric threads by bringing the needle up in the center of the next bar.

*Note: Weaving may also be worked by coming down into the middle of the 4 threads and proceeding as above.*

*Note: There will be a small thread showing on the back as you cross over from 1 bar to the next.*

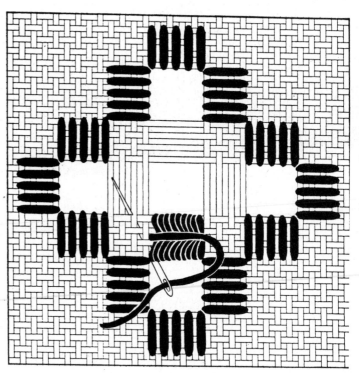

C

## HARDANGER PICOTS

A Picot is worked at the same time you work the weaving, when the bar is *half* woven.

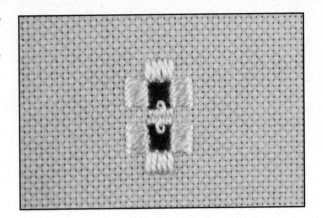

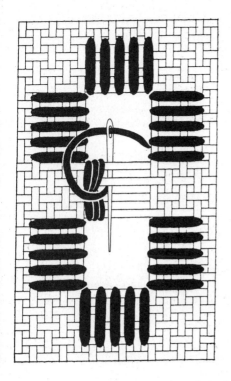

**A**

**B**

**1.** When you reach the center of the bar (about 4 weavings), put the needle halfway into the bar (so it comes toward you).

**2.** Wrap the thread over the needle, then under the end of the needle.

**3.** Pull the needle through and adjust the Picot until it lies securely at the outside edge of the bar. Bring the needle around the outside of the bar into the center.

**4.** Repeat for the Picot on the other side of the bar.

**5.** Continue weaving to the end of the bar.

# EYELET STITCH

The sample is worked on Zweigart® Hardanger with DMC® #8 and #12 Perle Cotton.

The Eyelet Stitch is used to fill square unworked areas, usually between Kloster Blocks. It *must* be worked before any cutting is done.

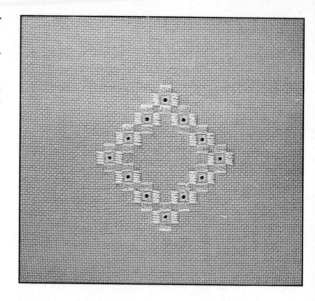

1. Fasten the thread under a Kloster Block on the wrong side of the fabric. Bring the needle to the front in the center hole at 1 and down into the corner hole at 2.

2. Come up at 1 and pull firmly.

3. Go down into the hole at 3 and up again at 1. Continue around the square.

## DOVE'S EYES (WEBS, LOOPS, FILETS)

The sample is made on Zweigart® Hardanger with DMC® #8 and #12 Perle Cotton.

This is one of the fillers that may be added to a piece of Hardanger embroidery to add a lacy appearance and can be worked with wrapped or woven bars or Kloster Blocks.

Dove's Eyes can be worked in a clockwise or counterclockwise direction; however, they must all be the same and cross exactly alike.

*Note: You must have 3 1/2 sides completed with weaving, wrapping, or Kloster Blocks before starting a Dove's Eye.*

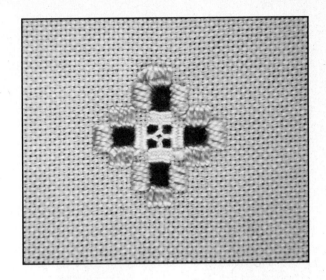

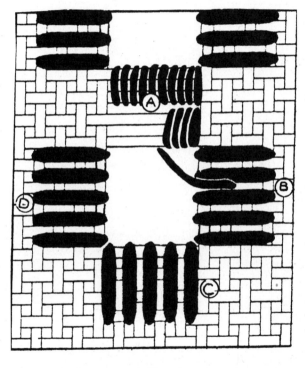

**A**

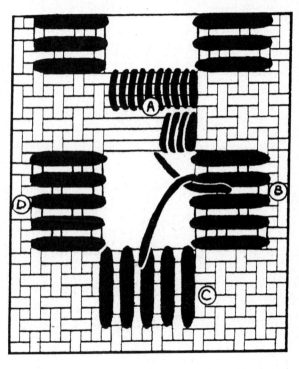

**B**

**1.** Working in a clockwise direction, put the thread that has just gone down into the wrapping of the first half of Bar A and come up into the open square and back down into the center of the Kloster Block to the right (B).

**2.** Return the thread to the open square, carrying the thread *over* the loop made from Bar A to the Kloster Block (C).

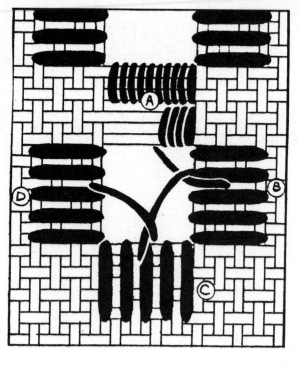

C

D

3. Repeat steps 1 and 2 over Kloster Block C and D. (Be sure to go *over* loops BC and CD.)

4. Slip the thread *under* the first loop (AB) coming from Kloster Block D. Weave the thread *down* into the half-wrapped Bar A and come up on the outside of the bar. Continue wrapping to the end.

## CROSS FILLING STITCH

The sample is worked on Zweigart® Hardanger with DMC® #5 Perle Cotton for the Kloster Blocks and #8 for the cross.

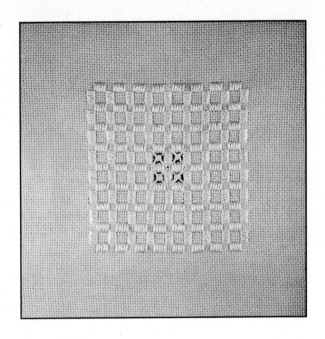

1. Work the Satin Stitch Kloster Blocks with #5 Perle Cotton. Cut out the center.

2. Place a long diagonal stitch from 1 to 2.

3. Make 4 twists around the long diagonal stitch, working toward the starting point (1). Run the needle behind the Kloster Block at the top.

4. Work a second long diagonal stitch from 3 to 4.

5. Make 2 twists to the center of the long diagonal stitch. Weave over and under the spokes 2 to 3 times.

6. Make 2 more twists, working toward 4, as before to complete the stitch.

## TULIP/SHIP MOTIF

The sample is worked on Zweigart® Hardanger with DMC® #5 Perle Cotton.

All Hardanger motifs are basically variations of the Satin Stitch (see page 51). This stitch is worked in 4 quarter sections or quadrants.

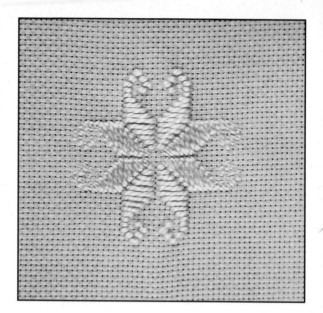

**A**

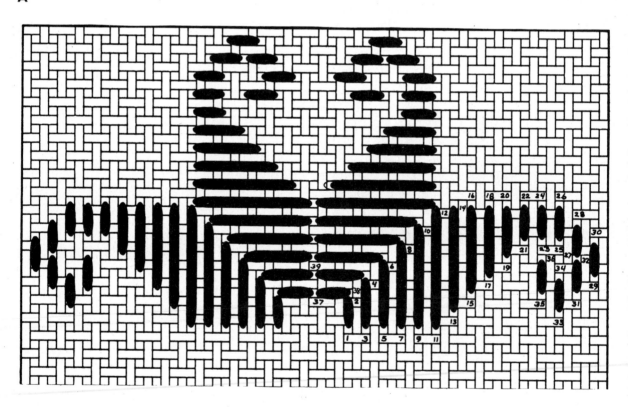

**1.** Follow steps 1 to 3 of the Star Motif (see page 72). Follow the Tulip/Ship Diagram A for the number and placement of the Satin Stitches.

**2.** When you complete Satin Stitch 35-36, slip the needle and thread *under* the completed Satin Stitches on the *wrong* side, coming to the front at 37 to work the second half of the first Tulip/Ship Motif quadrant.

*Note: This single quadrant can be used alone, in pairs as a half motif (as shown in Diagram A), or following Diagram B, worked with all 4 quadrants.*

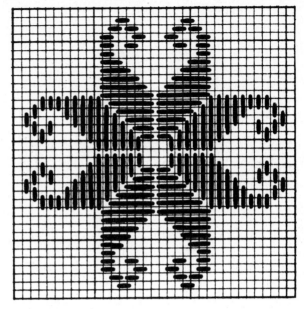

B

## TULIP/SHIP MOTIF, VARIATION 1.

The sample is worked on Zweigart® Hardanger with DMC® #5 Perle Cotton.
   This variation is worked in the same way as the Hardanger Tulip/Ship Motif.
   Follow *this* diagram exactly to achieve this variation.

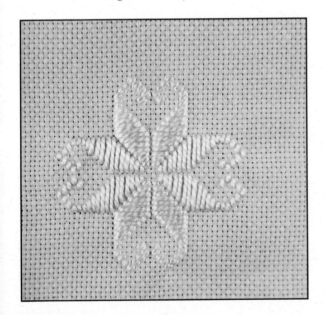

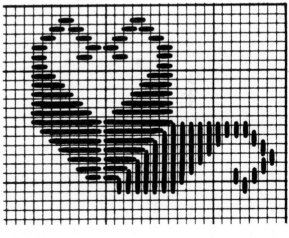

## TULIP/SHIP MOTIF, VARIATION 2.

The sample is worked on Zweigart® Hardanger with DMC® Perle Cotton.

This variation is worked in the same way as the Hardanger Tulip/Ship Motif (see pages 70–71).

Follow *this* diagram exactly to achieve this variation.

*Note: The Tulip/Ship Motifs may be made larger or smaller by varying the number and length of the Satin Stitches.*

 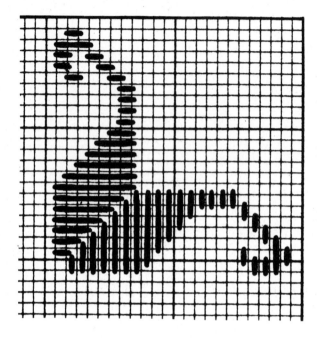

## STAR MOTIF (8-POINT STAR)

The sample is worked on Zweigart® Hardanger with DMC® Perle Cotton.

All Hardanger motifs are basically variations of the Satin Stitch (see page 51).

The Star Motif is made up of 8 points or petals that are worked separately from the center of the star to the outside points.

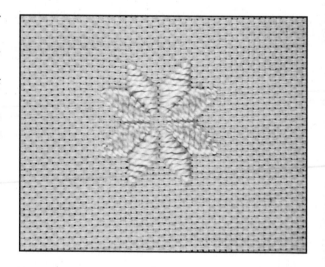

**1.** Locate the center hole in the space in which you will work the Star Motif (marked *x* on diagram). Count 2 holes to the right of the center hole (under 2 vertical fabric threads).

**2.** Bring the thread up in this hole (marked 1 on the diagram) and using the *stab* method (DO NOT SEW THIS MOTIF) come down at 2 (over 2 horizontal fabric threads). This completes the first Satin Stitch.

**3.** Continue working the Satin Stitches as shown on Diagram A. Notice that you increase the length of each stitch by 1 horizontal fabric thread until you finish stitch 9–10 (over 6 horizontal fabric threads).

**4.** Starting with stitch 11–12, decrease each stitch by 1 horizontal fabric thread at the bottom of the petal and maintaining a straight line at the top. The petal is complete when you reach stitch 17–18 and have worked 9 Satin Stitches.

**5.** Slip the needle and thread *under* these completed stitches on the *wrong* side, coming up at 18. Work the next petals in the same way as the first.

**6.** Diagram B shows the completed star shape. The center, unworked area (4 horizontal and 4 vertical fabric threads) can be left unworked or embellished with an Eyelet Stitch (see page 108).

*Note: The size of the Star Motif can be enlarged by increasing the number of stitches in each petal.*

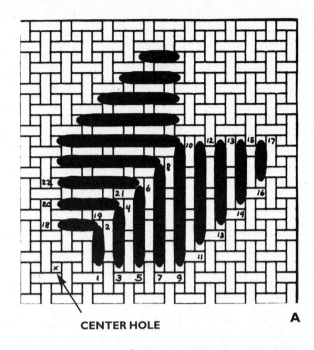

**CENTER HOLE**

**A**

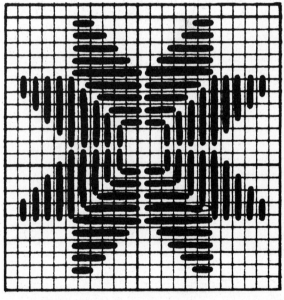

**B**

## HARDANGER, TREE PATTERN

The sample is worked on Zweigart® Hardanger with DMC® #5 Perle Cotton, #911 Cotton Floss (filler stitches), and Fil de Or (eyelets).

With some careful planning, you can work Hardanger in many shapes and designs. The Tree Pattern makes a lovely border for a piece of holiday linen.

The diagram is half of the tree pattern. The center is marked on the diagram. Remember to *repeat* the pattern on the left side to make a tree shape.

CENTER

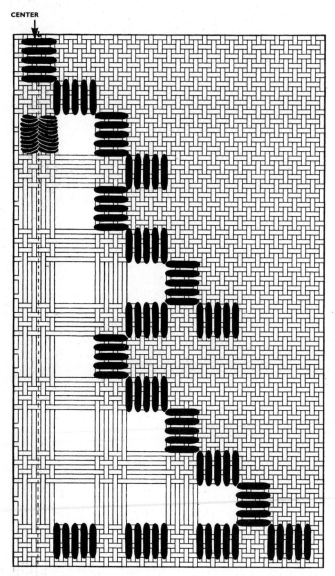

1. Starting at the center top, first work all the Satin Stitch blocks with the thicker thread. Do both sides, and follow the diagram very carefully. If the left side does not line up exactly with the right side, you will not be able to withdraw the threads.

2. Cut and pull out the fabric threads as indicated on the diagram. Be sure to trim close to the Satin Stitch blocks.

3. Work the (woven) bars, adding any Loop Stitches or Picots you may want to include as decorations or holiday ornaments.

# HEMSTITCH

This is a Drawn-Thread technique that requires the removal of some fabric threads. The remaining threads are then grouped to form patterns by lacing and/or knotting them together. It is used to make decorative bands on clothing or household linens.

Perle Cotton (Coton Perle) is best for this work.

## DIAMOND HEMSTITCH

The sample is worked on Zweigart® Brittany with DMC® #12 Perle Cotton.

This stitch works best as a border design.

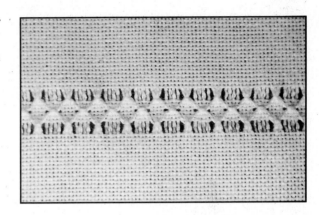

1. To start, remove 3 horizontal fabric threads, leave 6, remove 3 horizontal fabric threads.

2. Bring the thread up from the back at 1 and bring it down at 2 (over 4 vertical fabric threads), returning back to the front at 1.

A

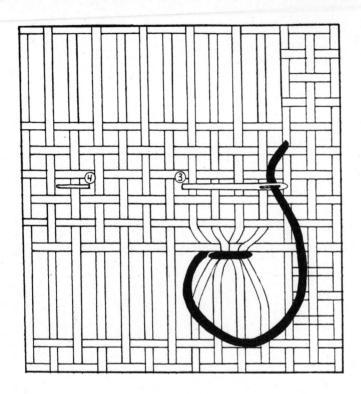

**3.** Pull this stitch firmly. Put the needle down at 3 (up over 3 horizontal fabric threads) and back to the front at 4 (under 4 vertical fabric threads to the left).

B

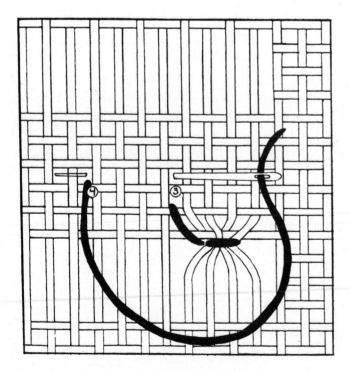

**4.** Pull this thread through the fabric to the front. Put the needle back into the fabric at 3 and return to the front at 4.

C

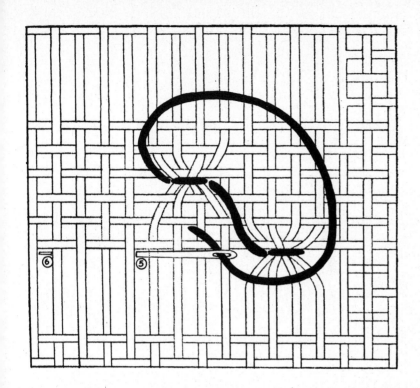

**5.** Pull this stitch firmly. Put the needle down at 5 (over 3 horizontal fabric threads) and back to the front at 6 (under 4 vertical threads to the left).

D

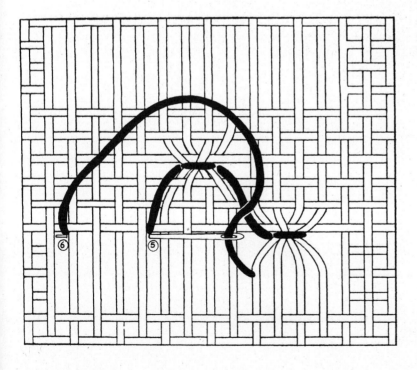

**6.** Put the needle back into 5 and return to the front at 6. Pull firmly.

E

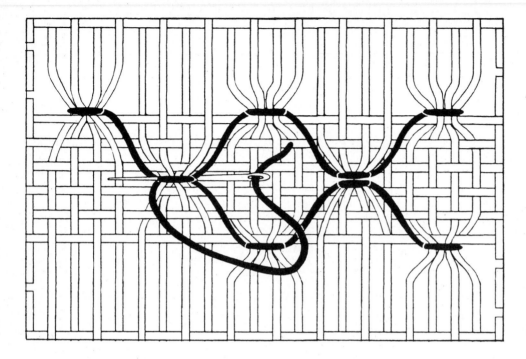

F

7. Repeat across the row.

8. *Turn the fabric around* and repeat to work the second row.

*Note: The connecting stitches are worked into the same holes as the first row.*

## LADDER HEMSTITCH

The sample is worked on 25-count Zweigart®
Dublin with DMC® #8 Perle Cotton.
   This stitch works up best as a border design.

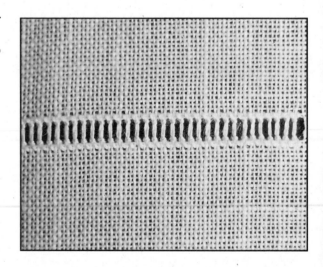

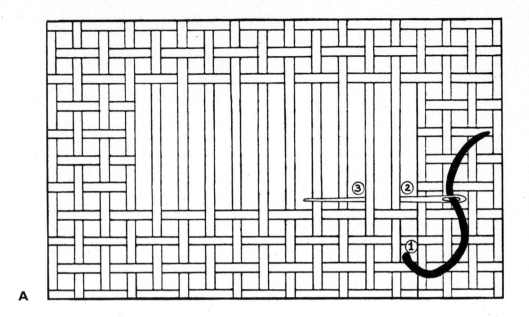

**A**

**1.** For this sample, remove 4 horizontal fabric threads (it will work with more threads removed). Weave the cut threads into the fabric at each side.

**2.** Bring the thread through to the front at 1 (2 horizontal fabric threads down from the removed threads). Put the needle in at 2 and back to the front at 3 (under 2 loose vertical threads to the left).

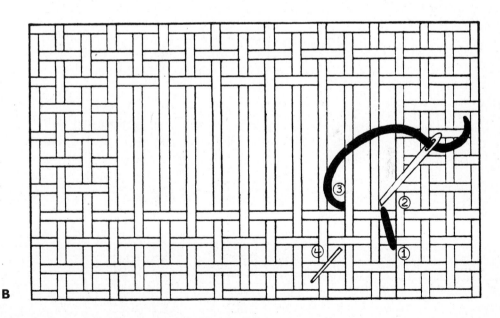

**B**

**3.** Pull this stitch with a medium-firm tug on the thread. Insert the needle back into 2 (over 2 vertical loose threads) and bring it back to the front at 4 (under 2 horizontal and 2 vertical fabric threads).

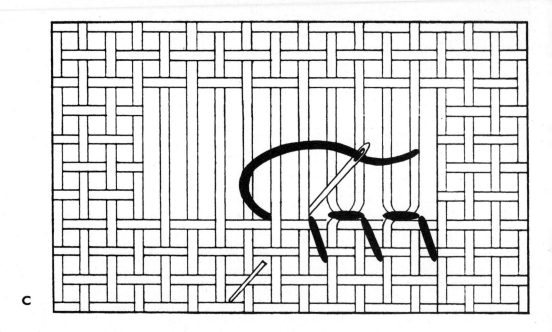

**C**

**4.** Repeat across to the end of the row.

**5.** *Turn the fabric around* and repeat with a row of stitches on the opposite edge of the space where the threads were removed.

*Note: Be careful to work your stitches over the corresponding pairs of loose threads on the opposite edge of the space where the first row of stitches was made. This will create the look of a ladder.*

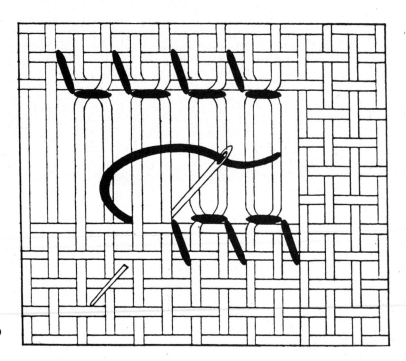

**D**

# TWISTED LADDER STITCH
(HEMSTITCH INTERLACED)

The sample is worked on 25-count Zweigart®
Lugana with DMC® #8 Perle Cotton.
   This stitch works best as a border design.

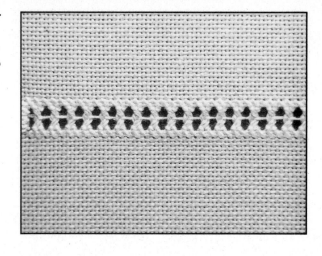

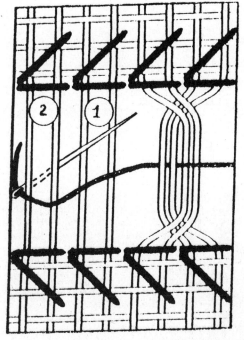

A

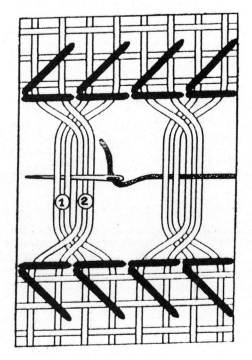

B

1. To start, remove the desired number of horizontal fabric threads. For this sample, 6 horizontal fabric threads are removed or withdrawn.

2. Work a row of Hemstitch (see "Ladder Hemstitch," page 78) along both edges of the withdrawn threads.

3. To make the twist, place the needle from left to right behind the second pair of threads (marked 2 on Diagram A) and over the first pair of threads (marked 1 on the diagram).

4. Twist pair 2 over pair 1 by turning the needle from right to left behind pair 1. Pull the lacing thread gently to lie firmly in the center of the twisted pairs of threads. Repeat across the row.

## ZIGZAG HEMSTITCH

The sample is worked on 32-count Zweigart®
Belfast with DMC® #12 Cotton Perle.

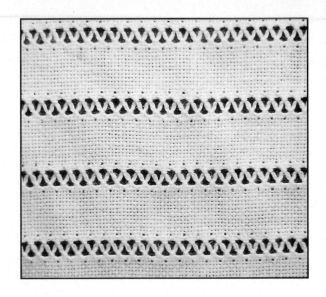

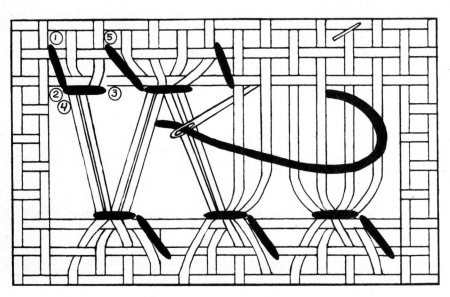

**1.** To begin, withdraw the desired number of fabric threads. In the sample, 4 horizontal threads were
withdrawn.

**2.** Following the diagram, work the Hemstitch along one edge of the withdrawn threads (1–2, 2–3, 3–4,
4–5, etc.). (See "Ladder Hemstitch," page 78.) Be sure that you have an even number of threads in each
group of threads that you catch together. The sample shows 4 threads in each group, but you can work
2 threads just as easily for a lighter effect.

**3.** Work the opposite edge as shown in the diagram. Note that the row begins and ends with a half group
of threads.

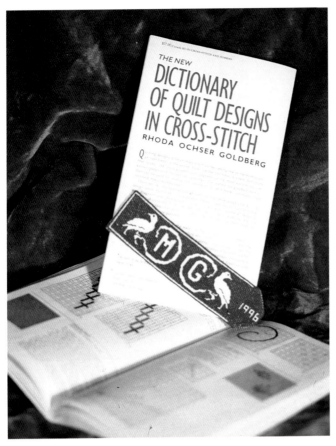

Assisi Embroidery Bookmark

Assisi Elephant Border Bread Cover

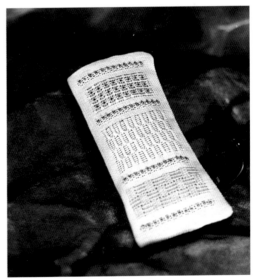

Dale's Pulled-Thread Eyeglass Case

Assisi Embroidery Towel

Napkin Rings

Blackwork Border Towel

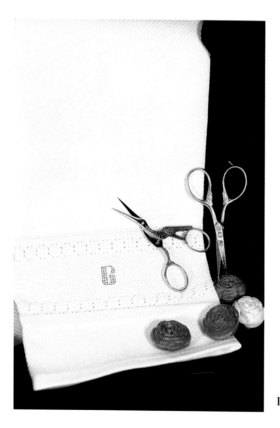

Darning Pattern Border Towel

Pulled Thread Alphabet Towel

Emily Rose Sampler

Assisi Embroidery Alphabet Sampler

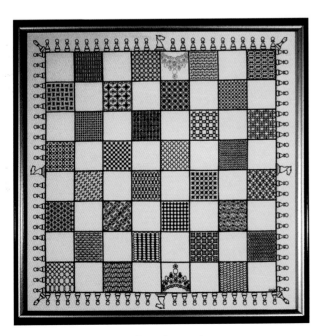

Chess Anyone?

Eyelet Alphabet Towel

Darning Pattern #2

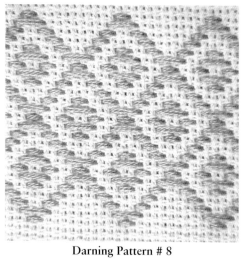

Darning Pattern # 8

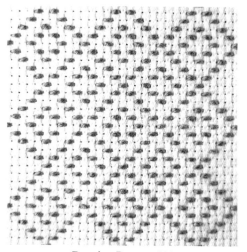

Darning Pattern #11

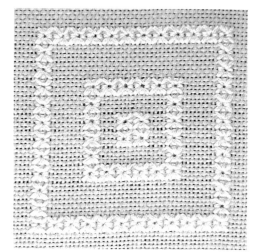

Star Stitch (small)

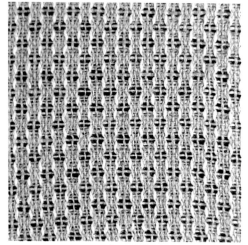

Window Filling

Small Chessboard Filling

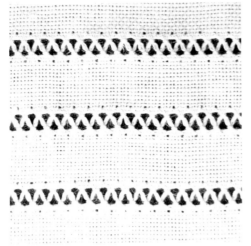

Zigzag Hemstitch

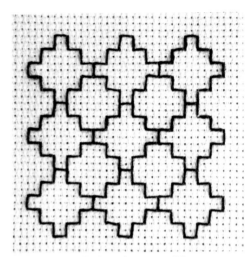

Blackwork Pattern #2

Blackwork Pattern #9

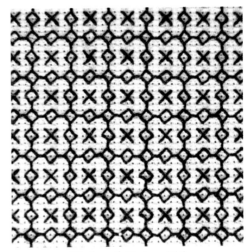

Blackwork Pattern #16

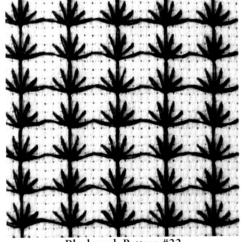

Blackwork Pattern #22

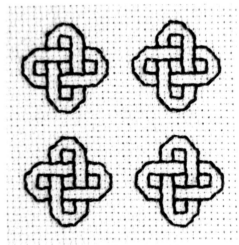

Blackwork Pattern #28

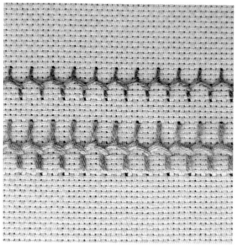

Cretan Stitch

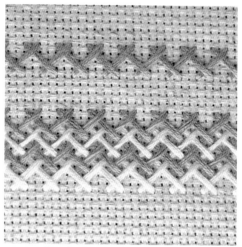

Herringbone (Plaited Gobelin)

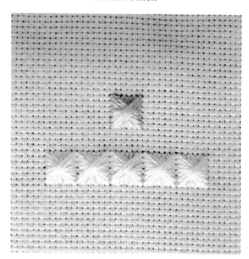

Rhodes Stitch

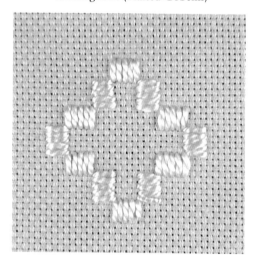

Hardanger Cutting "A"

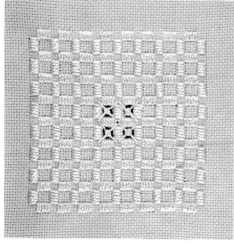

Hardanger (Cross Filling Stitch)

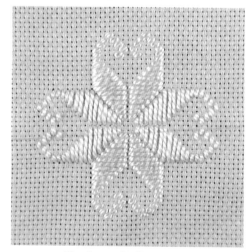

Hardanger Tulip (Var. 1)

Hardanger Tree

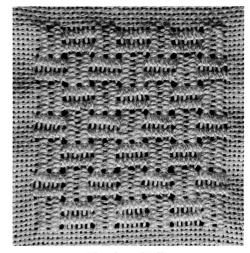

Chessboard Filling

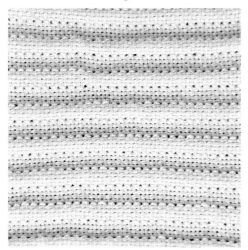

Double Backstitch

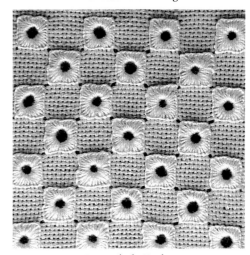

Buttonhole Eyelet

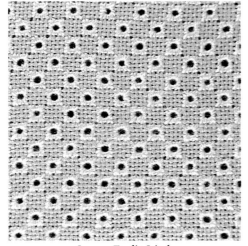

Square Eyelit Stitch

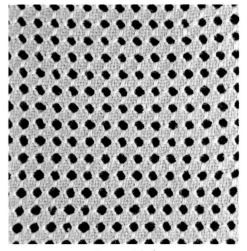

Faggot Stitch

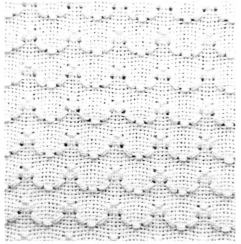

**Festoon 2**

**Greek Cross Stitch**

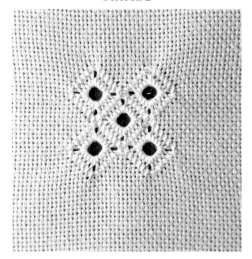

**Outlined Diamond Eyelet**

**Alphabet #2 (with Eyelet)**

**Alphabet #4 (Emily Rose)**

**Assisi Pattern #1 (Mythical Animal)**

# P

## PATTERN DARNING

This technique is a way of creating woven patterns by weaving running stitches in straight lines across evenweave fabric in a regular sequence of counted threads.

Samples of this work are found in Mexico, India, Scandinavia, and the former Slav countries.

It is often used to embellish ecclesiastical articles as well as clothing and household linens.

All kinds of Pattern Darning are reversible and can be worked horizontally, vertically, or diagonally.

In a Double Darning pattern, the fabric is covered completely and is usually worked in two colors.

This technique is worked on evenweave fabric using a thread that is approximately the same weight and thickness as the thread of the fabric. Embroidery floss or Perle Cotton are the most common threads used; however, if you use a heavy, coarse fabric, one or more strands of crewel yarn can be used.

### DARNING PATTERN #1

The sample is worked on Zweigart® Aida #14 with DMC® Cotton Floss.

This pattern is worked in horizontal rows, over 3 and under 2 vertical fabric threads.

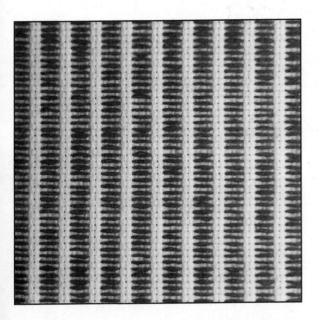
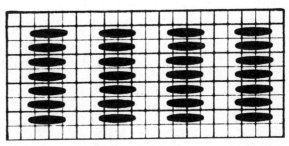

## DARNING PATTERN #2

The sample is worked on Zweigart® Aida #18 with DMC® Cotton Floss.

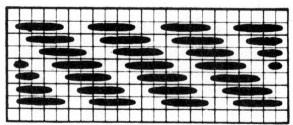

## DARNING PATTERN #3

The sample is worked on Zweigart® Aida #18 with DMC® Cotton Floss.

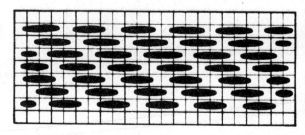

## DARNING PATTERN #4

The sample is worked on Fiddlers Cloth #14 with DMC® Cotton Floss.
   This is a simple stitch, over 2 and under 2 vertical fabric threads.

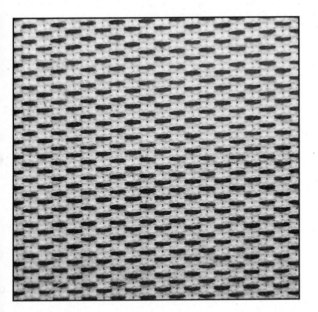 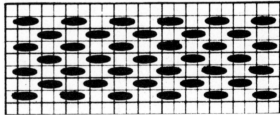

## DARNING PATTERN #5

The sample is worked on Fiddlers Cloth #14 with DMC® Cotton Floss.

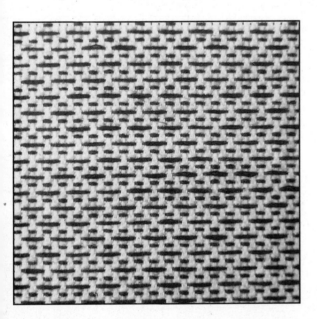 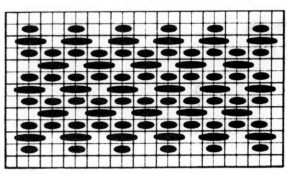

## DARNING PATTERN #6

The sample is worked on Zweigart® Aida #14 with DMC® Cotton Floss.
This pattern is worked in vertical rows.

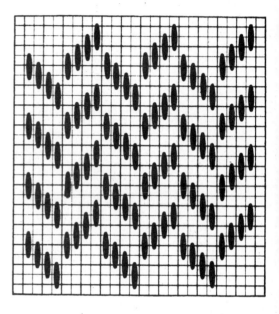

## DARNING PATTERN #7

The sample is worked on Zweigart® Aida #14 with DMC® Cotton Floss.

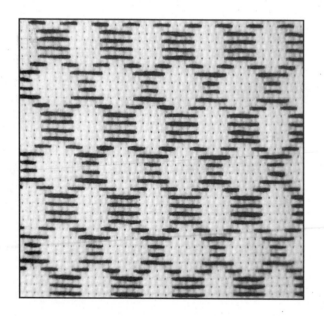
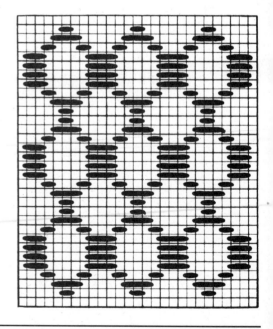

## DARNING PATTERN #8

The sample is worked on the border of a Charles Craft towel; however, it can be worked on any other even-weave fabric.

(For instructions on how to make the towel border, including another alphabet, see "Projects," page 152.)

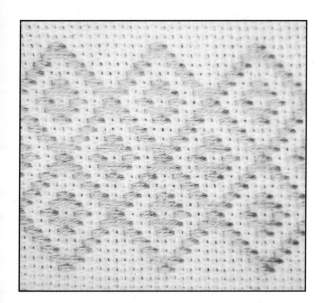 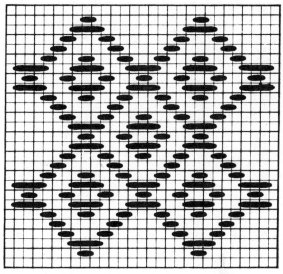

## DARNING PATTERN #9

The sample is worked on Zweigart® Aida #14 with DMC® Cotton Floss (use 6-ply).

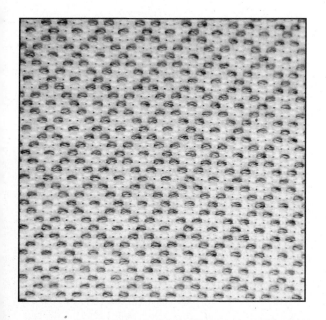 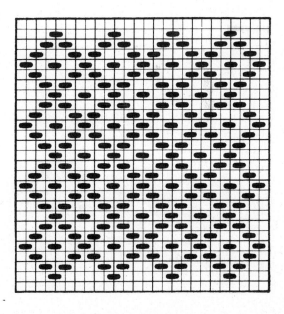

## DARNING PATTERN #10

The sample is worked on Fiddlers Cloth #14 with DMC® Cotton Floss.

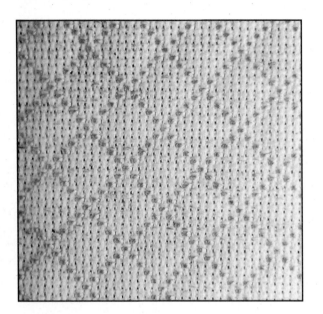

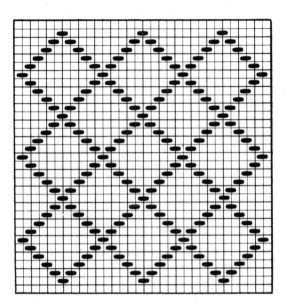

## DARNING PATTERN #11

The sample is worked on Zweigart® Aida #14 with DMC® Cotton Floss.
Notice that this is the same pattern as #10 with the addition of a diamond shape in the center.

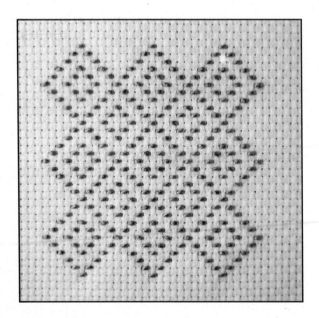

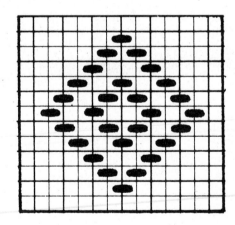

## DARNING PATTERN #12

The sample is worked on Fiddlers Cloth #14 with DMC® Cotton Floss.
   Notice that this is another variation of Darning Pattern #10.

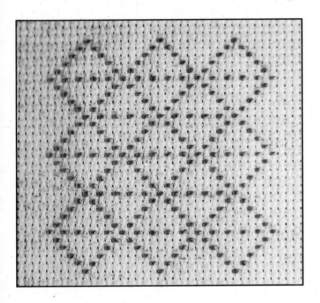
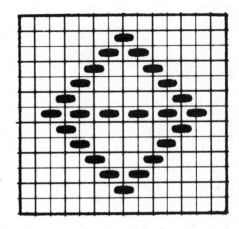

## DARNING PATTERN #13

The sample is worked on Zweigart® Aida #14 with DMC® Cotton Floss.
   This is another variation of Darning Pattern #10.

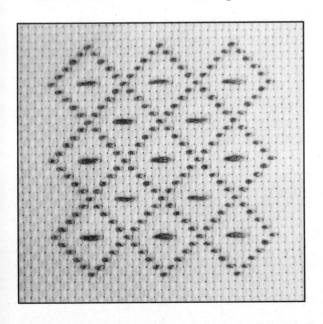
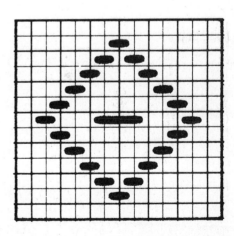

## DARNING PATTERN #14

The sample is worked on Zweigart® Aida #14 with DMC® Cotton Floss.

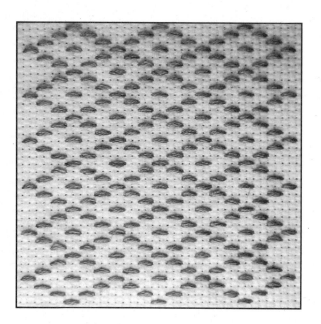

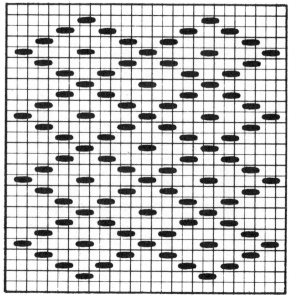

## DARNING PATTERN #15

The sample is worked on Zweigart® Aida #14 with DMC® Cotton Floss.

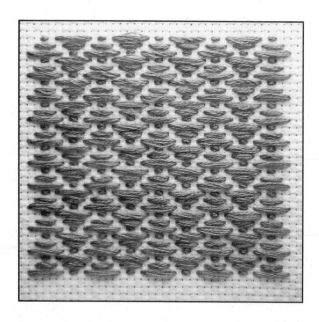

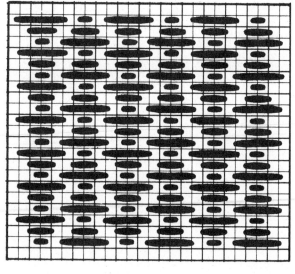

## DARNING PATTERN #16

The sample is worked on Fiddlers Cloth #14 with DMC® Cotton Floss.
This pattern is worked vertically.

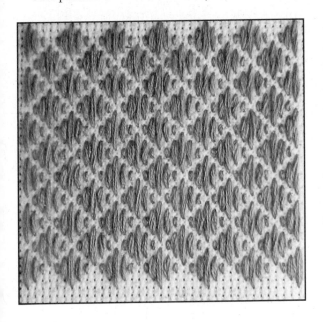 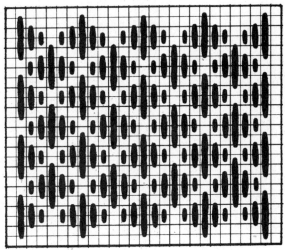

# PULLED-THREAD

Pulled-Thread is a type of Counted-Thread embroidery in which the fabric threads are drawn together by pulling the stitches tightly to from planned open spaces that give the fabric the look of lace. It is usually worked with the same color fabric and thread to create this illusion.

Pulled-Thread is always worked on an evenweave fabric (such as linen, cotton, Aida, Hardanger, or Congress Cloth) using a tapestry (blunt-tip) needle. The thread should be the same weight as the fabric threads.

If you outline the areas of Pulled-Thread work, you can use a sharp-tip needle and any of the surface stitches (such as Backstitch, Outline Stitch, or Chain Stitch). I usually use 6-ply Cotton Floss or Perle Cotton size #3 to #12. Linen threads, flower threads, and silk threads also work very well.

Samples of Pulled-Thread embroidery are found all over the world.

**Pulled-Thread Tension.** When working Pulled-Thread, the pattern is often determined or changed by the amount of tension or pull exerted on the stitch.

Diagrams A through C show the different tensions and how each will distort the fabric threads.

Many stitches can be worked with no pull (A), medium pull (B), or firm pull (C). Satin and Eyelet Stitches are good examples of this. Most of the Double Backstitches are worked with either no pull or medium pull, and the majority of the other Pulled-Thread stitches are worked with firm pull or tight tension.

As you work the stitches, always look at how the pull or tension is distorting the fabric.

Always remember when working Pulled-Thread stitches that the fabric threads must be pulled from both sides of the stitch or the stitch will distort and not look correct.

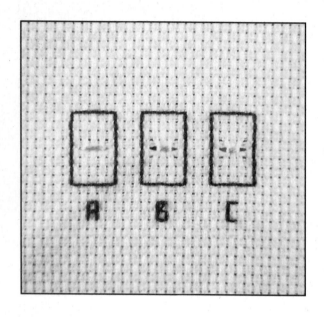

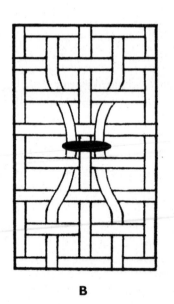

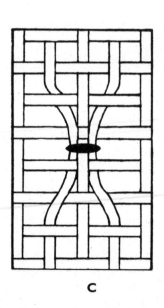

A                    B                    C

## ALGERIAN FILLING

The sample is worked on 18-count Zweigart® Aida with DMC® Cotton Floss.

This stitch is based on the Satin Stitch (see page 51). It is primarily used to cover large areas. A firm pull will result in a lacy stitch, and little or no pull will produce a more solid effect.

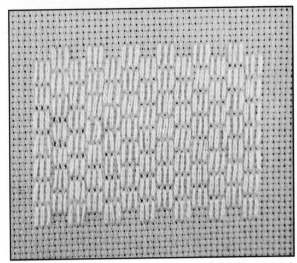

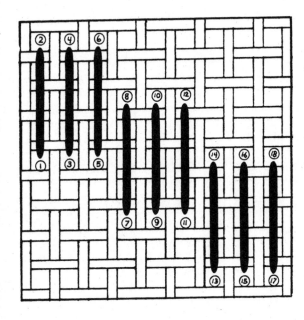

**A**

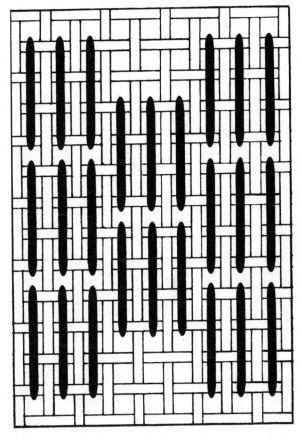

**B**

**1.** This stitch should be worked on the diagonal following the numbers on Diagram A. Start with 1–2, 3–4, and 5–6, forming a Satin Stitch block of 3 stitches over 4 horizontal fabric threads.

**2.** The next block begins 6 horizontal fabric threads down and 1 vertical fabric thread to the right (7–8, 9–10, 11–12). Continue in this way, completing all Satin Stitch blocks (13–14, 15–16, 17–18, etc.).

*Note: Diagram B shows the allover pattern.*

## BACKSTITCH

The sample is worked on 18-count Zweigart® Aida with DMC® #8 Perle Cotton. *Use no pull tension.*

This is the basic stitch used for outlining an area to be filled with Pulled-Thread, Blackwork, or Embroidery Stitches.

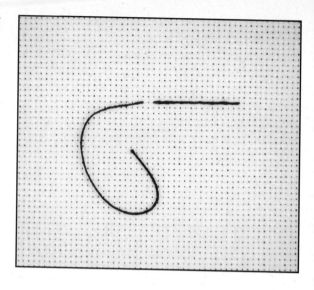

**1.** To work a row, come up from the back at 1 and down over 2 vertical fabric threads.

**2.** Go to the left under 4 vertical fabric threads, coming up at 2, and go down over 2 vertical fabric threads.

**3.** Repeat step 2 across the row.

*Note: This stitch can be worked horizontally, vertically, diagonally, or even around a curve. (See Whipped Backstitch Diagrams A–B–C.)*

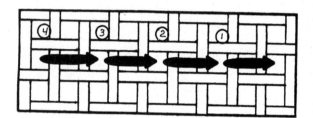

## BACKSTITCH, WHIPPED

The sample is worked on 14-count Zweigart® Aida with DMC® #8 Perle Cotton.

This variation of the Backstitch produces a heavier line. *Use no pull tension.*

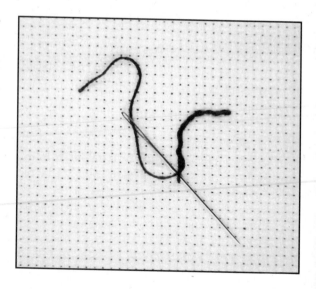

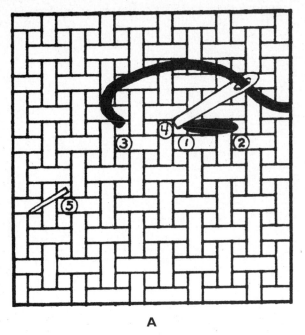

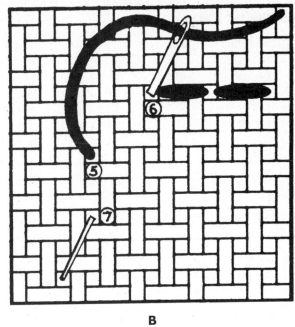

**A**

**B**

1. Work your Backstitches according to Diagram A (horizontal), and B (diagonal, 5–6, and vertical, 7–5).

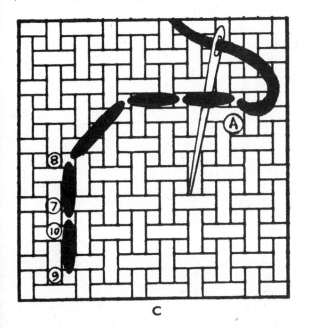

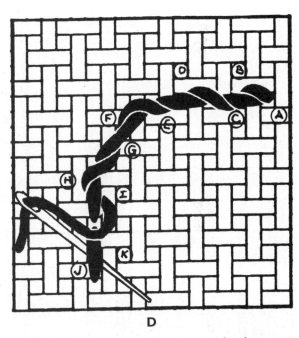

**C**

**D**

2. Starting with a new thread, bring the needle to the front at A on Diagram C. Now put the needle under the thread of the first stitch, being careful not to pierce the fabric.

3. Put the needle under the next and subsequent stitches in the same way without piercing the fabric.

## CHESSBOARD FILLING

The sample is worked on 25-count Zweigart® Lugana with DMC® #8 Perle Cotton.

This stitch consists of double rows of Satin Stitches that create horizontal and vertical rectangular blocks. The diagram shows each block worked with 7 Satin Stitches over 3 threads of fabric.

**1.** Following the diagram, start at 1–2, working vertically until 7 horizontal Satin Stitches are completed.

**2.** Begin the next row of horizontal Satin Stitches at 15–16 and complete the rectangular block.

**3.** To start the next block of vertical stitches, begin at A–B, working horizontally to complete the vertical Satin Stitches as shown in the diagram.

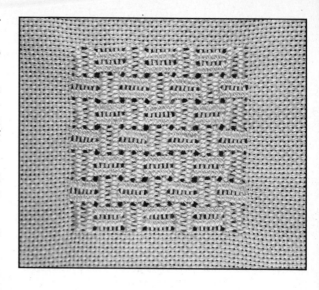

*Note: Pull all stitches with a firm tension to create the open effect.*

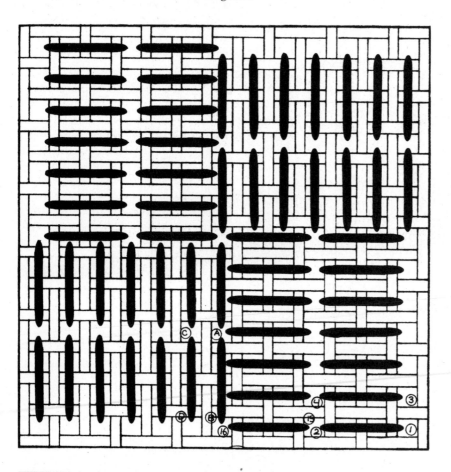

## COIL FILLING

The sample is worked with 28-count Zweigart®
Brittany and DMC® #12 Perle Cotton.

This stitch is formed by making clusters of 3 vertical Satin Stitches worked together over the same
threads with an even number of fabric threads left
unworked between each cluster of stitches.

The sample is worked over 4 horizontal fabric
threads with 4 vertical fabric threads between each
cluster. *Use a firm pull.*

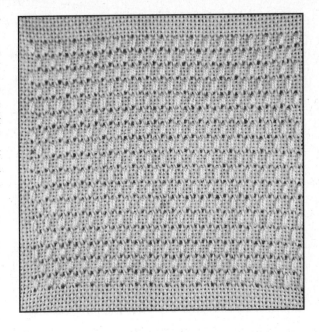

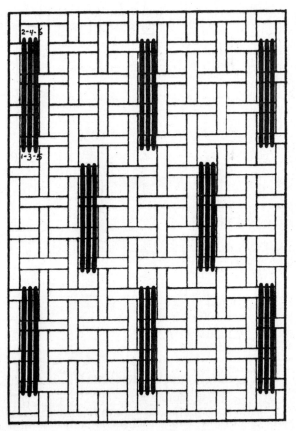

1. Begin at 1–2, 3–4, 5–6. This is the first cluster.

2. Continue in the same manner across the row.

*Note: Secure the thread at the end of each row.*

3. Starting again at the left side, work the second row.

## CUSHION FILLING

The sample is worked on 25-count Zweigart® Dublin with DMC® #8 Perle Cotton.

The name of this stitch comes from the appearance of the puffy or cushionlike ovals produced by using a *very firm pull* or tension.

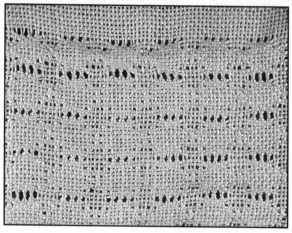

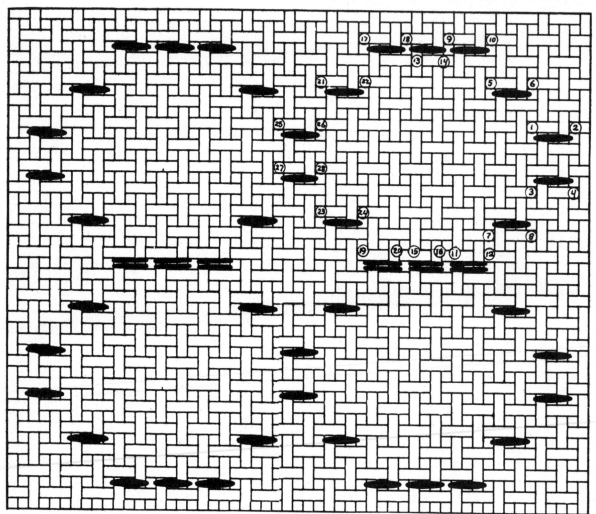

1. Bring the needle up at 1, down at 2 (over 2 vertical fabric threads), up at 3 (under 2 horizontal and 2 vertical fabric threads), and down at 4 (over 2 vertical fabric threads).

2. Now you *must* follow the numbers carefully. Bring the needle up at 5 (under 4 vertical and 4 horizontal fabric threads) and down over 2 vertical fabric threads at 6.

3. Continue following the numbers to 27–28. Notice that you jump from top to bottom for every pair of stitches.

4. The second puff or cushion continues across the row with 25–26 becoming 1–2 of the next cushion.

5. For the second row, note that 9–10 will share the same holes as 11–12 of the previous row. Other stitches will share holes as well, as shown.

## DIAGONAL RAISED BAND FILLING #1

The sample is worked on 25-count Zweigart® Lugana with DMC® #12 Perle Cotton.

   This stitch is composed of Upright Crosses worked on the diagonal with a *firm* tension.

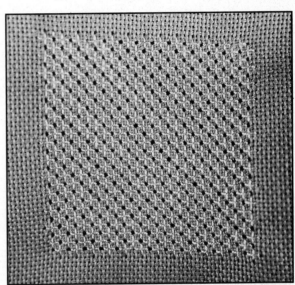

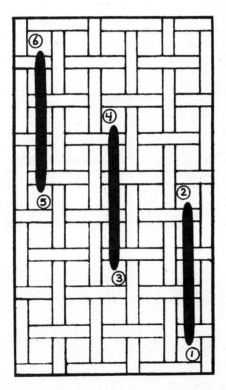

A

1. Following Diagram A, bring the thread to the front at 1 and down at 2 (4 threads up). Bring the needle out at 3 and down at 4. Continue across the area to be filled.

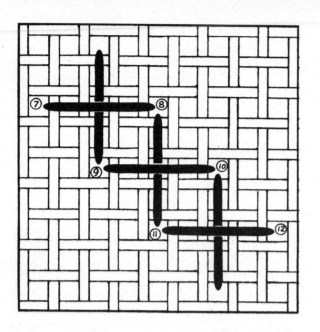

**2.** Next, make the crosses by bringing the needle up from the back at 7 (2 fabric threads down and 2 fabric threads to the left). Bring it down at 8 and up at 9, down at 10 and up at 11, and so forth. Diagram B shows the completed row of Upright Cross Stitches.

**3.** Diagram C shows rows of the Cross-Stitches worked closely together.

**B**

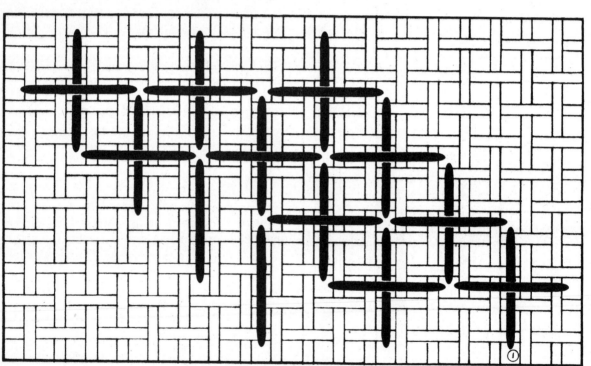

**C**

## DIAGONAL RAISED BAND FILLING #2
### (DIAGONAL CROSS FILLING)

The sample is worked on 25-count Zweigart®
Lugana with DMC® #8 Perle Cotton.

This stitch is worked exactly as Diagonal Raised
Band Filling #1, but over 6 fabric threads. This
stitch leaves 6 fabric threads between the diagonal
rows of stitches.

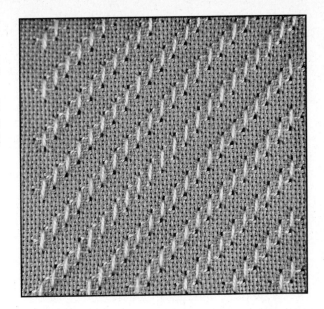

*Note: Start each new row with a new thread.*

**1.** The Diagonal Raised Band Stitches are worked in 2 steps, with the vertical stitches in the row worked
first. These are marked with numbers on the diagram, next page.

**2.** The horizontal stitches (also called the Return Journey) are then worked, completing the crosses. These
are marked with letters.

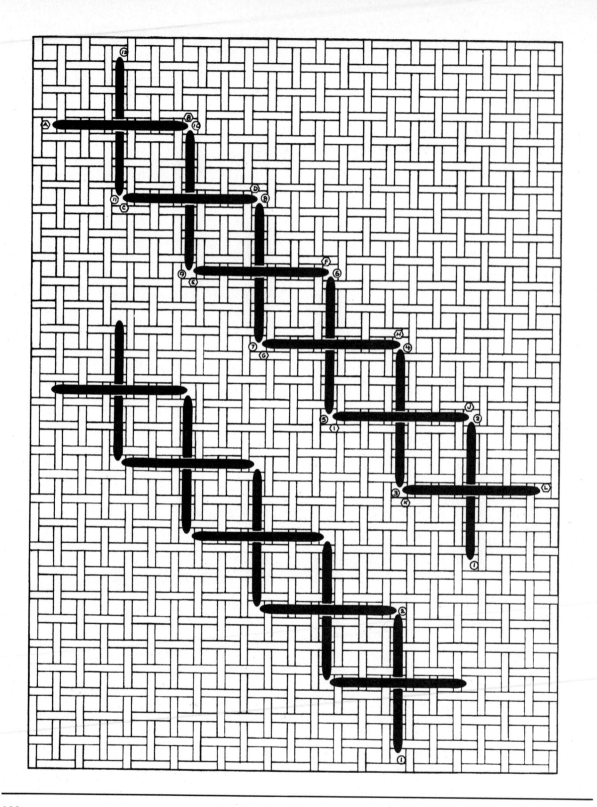

## DIAMOND FILLING #1

The sample is worked on 28-count Zweigart® Brittany with DMC® #8 Perle Cotton.

The Diamond Filling Stitch consists of Double Backstitches (see page 105) worked in stepped lines that make zigzag rows. Two rows of the zigzag pattern make a diamond pattern.

The diamonds can be worked with more or less steps and over 2, 3, or more vertical fabric threads. Always work over the same number of fabric threads throughout.

*This stitch requires a firm pull.* The broken lines on the diagram show the direction of the thread on the back or reverse side.

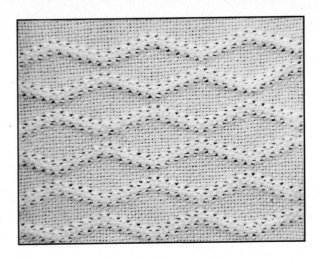

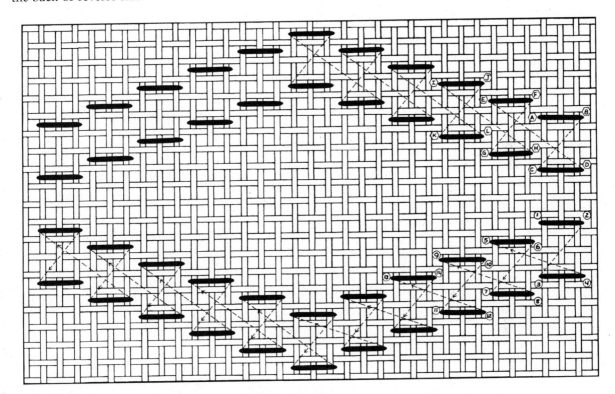

1. Begin at 1–2 (over 3 vertical fabric threads).

2. Come up at 3 (diagonally under 3 vertical and horizontal fabric threads) and down at 4 (over 3 vertical fabric threads).

3. Return to the front at 5 (diagonally under 6 vertical and 2 horizontal fabric threads) and down at 6 (over 3 vertical fabric threads).

4. Continue in this way, following the diagram, until the first zigzag is complete.

5. The second row begins at A–B and is worked in the same way as the first row.

## DIAMOND FILLING #2

The sample is worked on 28-count Zweigart® Brittany with DMC® #8 Perle Cotton.

This diagram shows a variation of the Diamond Filling Stitch with the Double Backstitches worked over 2 threads.

Follow the general directions for the Diamond Filling Stitch using this diagram. *Use a firm pull.*

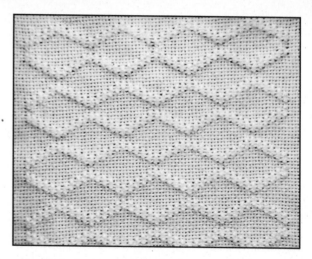

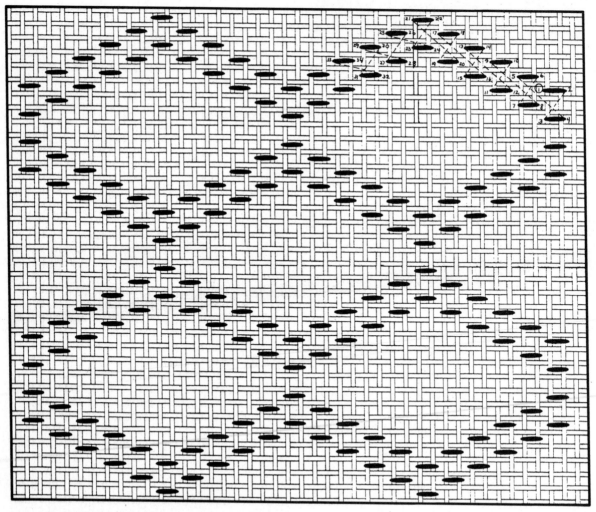

## DOUBLE BACKSTITCH

The sample is worked on 25-count Zweigart®
Lugana with DMC® #8 Perle Cotton.

Double Backstitches are used as a border or for
parallel lines as well as a base for other stitches. (For
example, see "Diamond Filling #1," page 103.)

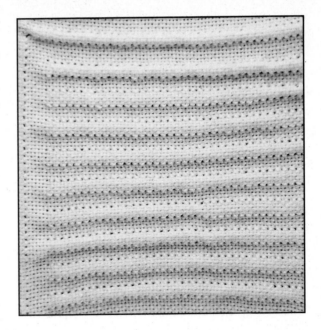

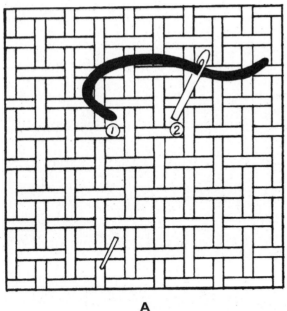

**A**

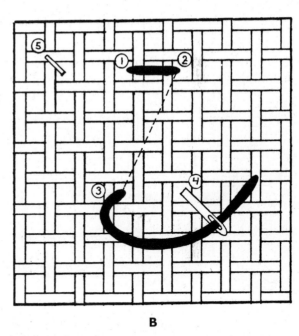

**B**

1. Bring the needle to the front at 1 and down at 2
(2 vertical fabric threads to the right). Return to the
front at 3 (4 fabric threads down and 2 to the left).

2. Go down with the needle at 4 (2 vertical fabric
threads to the right) and return to the front at 5
(4 horizontal and vertical fabric threads up and to
the left).

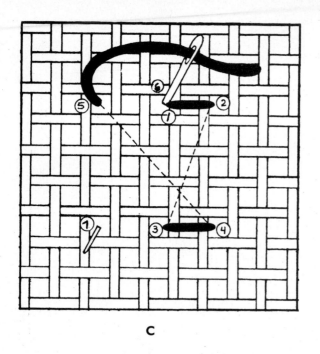

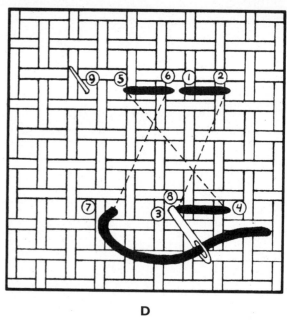

C

D

**3.** Place the needle down at 6 (2 vertical fabric threads to the right) and bring it to the front at 7 (4 horizontal fabric threads down and 2 vertical threads to the left).

**4.** Insert the needle at 8 and bring it to the front at 9. *Note the formation of the crosses on the reverse side.*

**5.** Continue in this manner across the row.

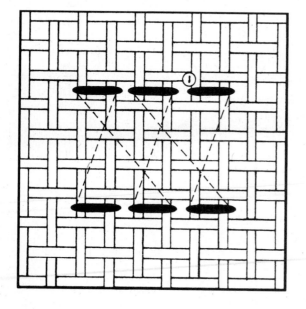

E

## DOUBLE STITCH FILLING

The sample is worked on 25-count Zweigart®
Lugana with DMC® #8 Perle Cotton.

Some stitches are the same as the reverse side of
another stitch. The Double Stitch is an example of
this; it is the same as the reverse side of the Window
Filling Stitch and it is worked with a *firm pull*.

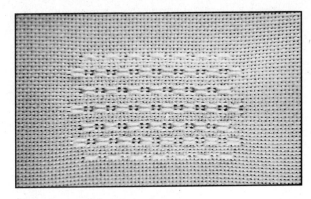

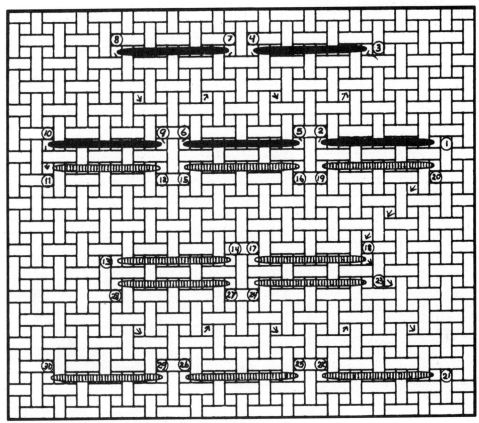

**1.** Come up from the back at 1 and go down over
5 vertical fabric threads at 2.

**2.** Go back under 2 vertical and 4 horizontal fabric
threads, coming up at 3, and go down over 5 vertical fabric threads at 4. Continue in this way across
the row. (These are the solid black stitches on the
diagram.)

**3.** To start the second row, using the same thread,
follow the shaded stitches on the diagram, coming
up from the back under 1 horizontal fabric thread
at 11 and down over 5 vertical fabric threads at 12.
Continue in this way, following the numbers on the
diagram.

# EYELET STITCHES

Eyelet Stitches are simply Satin Stitches (see page 51), all worked into a single center hole. The firmer the pull, the larger the hole in the center will be.

These stitches form a square when worked over an even number of vertical and horizontal fabric threads. The number of fabric threads determines the size of the stitch. These stitches may be worked as a Hardanger Eyelet by coming *up* in the center hole.

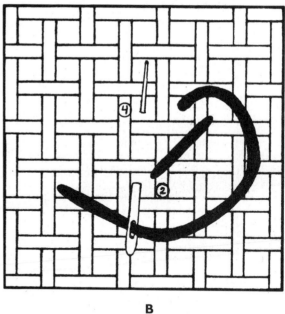

## (SQUARE EYELET, EYELET HOLES).

The sample is worked on 25-count Zweigart® Lugana with DMC® Floss (used 2-ply).

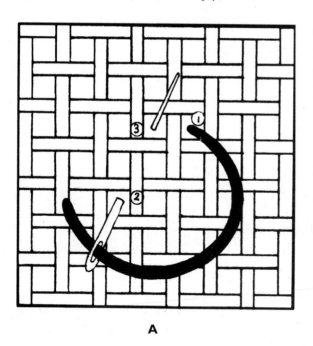

**A**

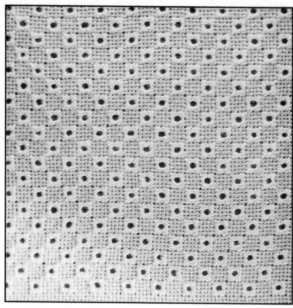

**B**

**1.** Bring the thread to the front at 1 and insert the needle down at 2 (2 horizontal and 2 vertical fabric threads to the left). Bring the needle to the front at 3 (2 horizontal and 1 vertical fabric threads to the right).

**2.** Insert the needle back into 2 and bring it to the front at 4 (up under 2 horizontal fabric threads).

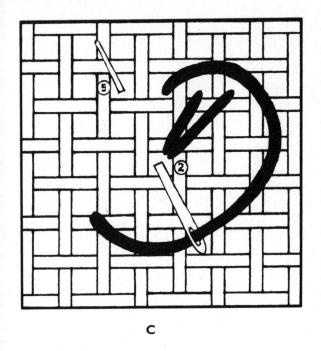

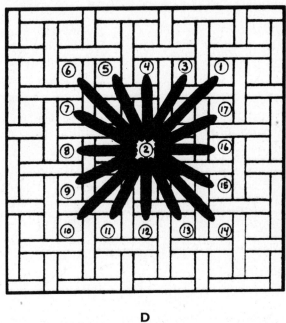

C

D

**3.** Insert the needle back into 2 and bring it up at 5 (2 horizontal and 1 vertical fabric threads to the left).

**4.** Continue working counterclockwise according to the numbers on the diagrams until the square is complete.

*Note:* You can work over any even number of horizontal and vertical fabric threads to form larger squares.

## BARRED BUTTONHOLE EYELET.

The sample is worked on 25-count Zweigart® Lugana with DMC® Ecru Floss (2 strands).

Basically, all Eyelet Stitches are Satin Stitches with all the legs worked into a single, center hole. This stitch differs from all the others in that a Buttonhole or Blanket Stitch is used in place of the Satin Stitch.

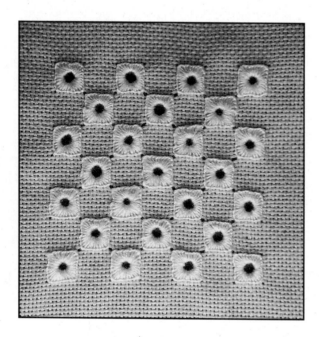

1. All the stitches begin at the center hole (1).

2. Work all the stitches as Buttonhole Stitches, following the numbers on the diagram. Work in a counterclockwise direction if you are right-handed and clockwise if you are left-handed.

*Note: This stitch may be worked over more or fewer fabric threads, but always in a square shape.*

## DIAMOND EYELET.

The sample is worked on 25-count Zweigart® Lugana with DMC® Ecru Floss (2 strands).

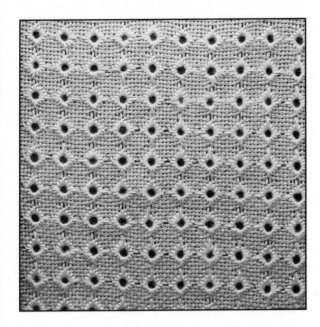

**1.** Bring the thread to the front at 1 and down at 2 (over 4 horizontal fabric threads).

**2.** Bring the needle back up at 1 (under 1 vertical and 3 horizontal fabric threads) and down at 3.

**3.** Continue working clockwise, following the numbers on the diagram.

## DOUBLE-CROSS EYELET.

The sample is worked on 25-count Zweigart® Lugana with DMC® Cotton Floss (2 strands).

This stitch forms a double cross (2 horizontal and 2 vertical fabric threads) in the center of the stitch. *It does not have a single large center hole as with most eyelet stitches, but is still considered to be an eyelet stitch.*

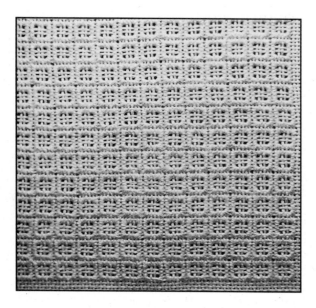

**1.** Bring the thread to the front at 1 and down at 2 (over 2 horizontal fabric threads).

**2.** Bring the needle up at 3 (under 2 horizontal and 1 vertical fabric threads) and down at 4 (over 2 horizontal fabric threads).

**3.** Working clockwise and following the diagram, bring the needle up at 5 and go back down into hole 4. Continue until this corner is complete.

**4.** Start the lower right-hand corner at 9. Continue as before until all 4 corners are complete.

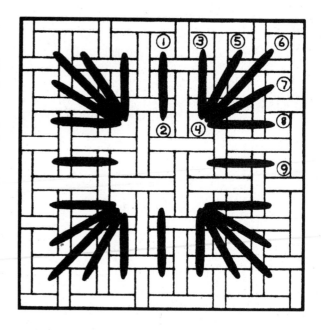

## EYE VARIATION.

The sample is worked on 25-count Zweigart®
Lugana with DMC® #5 Perle Cotton.

This stitch is complicated and requires some
practice before a regular rhythm can be established.
If you want a clear, firm look, it is recommended
that you work each stitch *twice* (1–2, then 1–2
again).

**1.** Bring the thread up at 1 and
down at 2 (over 3 vertical fabric
threads). *Repeat 1–2.*

**2.** Come back into hole 1 (now
called 3 on the diagram) and go
down into 4 (over 1 vertical and
4 horizontal fabric threads).
*Repeat 3–4.*

**3.** Bring the needle up at 5 (under
1 horizontal and 4 vertical fabric
threads) and down at 6 (over 3 vertical and 3 horizontal fabric
threads). *Repeat 5–6.*

**4.** Bring the needle up again at 5
(now called 7) and down at 8 (over
1 horizontal and 4 vertical fabric
threads). *Repeat 7–8.*

**5.** Bring the needle up at 9 and
down at 10. Continue, following
the numbers on the diagram until
the stitch is complete.

**Note:** *A single cross is formed in
the center.*

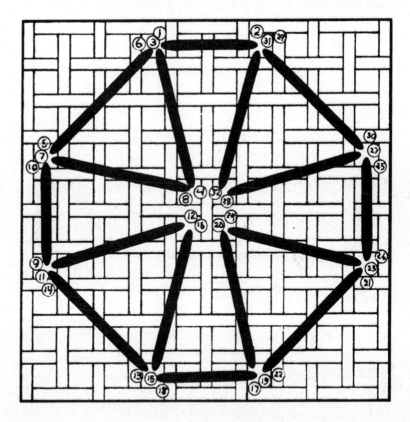

## HALF-DIAMOND EYELET.

The sample is worked on 25-count Zweigart® Lugana with DMC® #5 Perle Cotton.

 This stitch is worked with a *firm pull* to form a distinct center hole. It may be worked as shown on the diagram or turned upside down (with the point facing up).

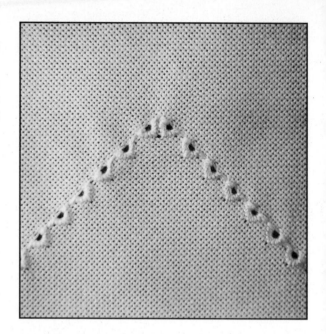

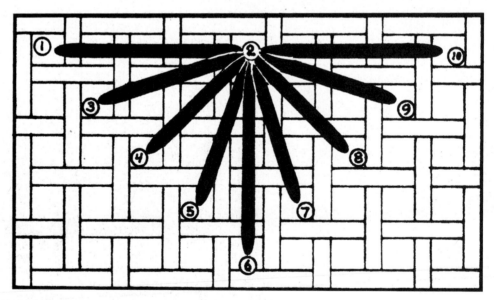

1. Bring the needle up at 1 and down at 2 (over 4 vertical fabric threads).

2. Bring the needle up at 3 (under 1 horizontal and 3 vertical fabric threads) and back down into the center hole (2).

3. Return to the front at 4 and continue around in a counterclockwise direction according to the diagram.

## HEXAGONAL EYELET (HEX EYELET).

The sample is worked on 25-count Zweigart®
Lugana with DMC® #8 Perle Cotton.

Work each stitch twice with a *firm* pull to form a
distinct center hole and a delicate open pattern.

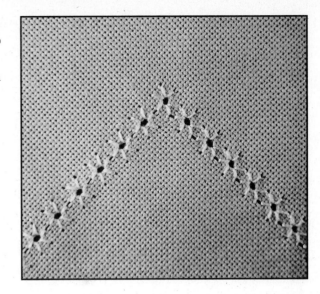

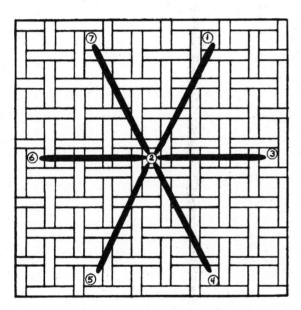

**1.** Bring the needle up at 1 and down into the center hole at 2 (over 2 vertical and 4 horizontal fabric
threads). *Repeat 1–2.*

**2.** Working clockwise, bring the needle up at 3
(under 4 vertical fabric threads) and down at 2.

**3.** Continue in this manner, *repeating each stitch,*
following the numbers on the diagram.

## ITALIAN EYELET.

The sample is worked on 25-count Zweigart® Lugana with DMC® #8 Perle Cotton *using a firm pull*.

This is a dense filling stitch produced by working horizontal rows of overlapping Star Stitches (see page 145).

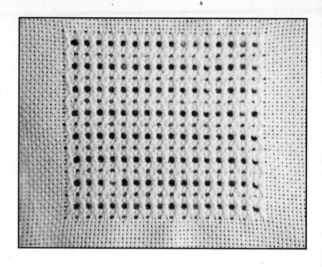

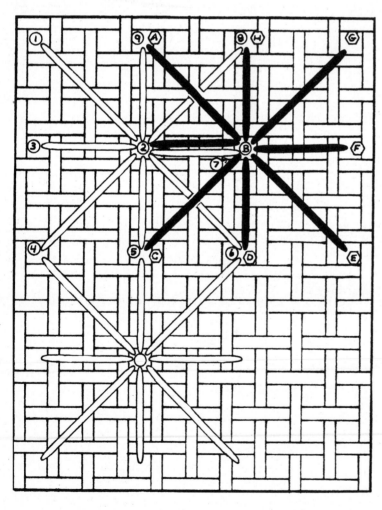

**1.** Following the white stitches on the diagram, begin the first eyelet stitch by coming up from the back at 1 and going down over 3 horizontal and 3 vertical fabric threads at 2 (the center hole).

**2.** Working counterclockwise, come up at 3 (under 3 vertical fabric threads) and go back down at 2.

**3.** Continue around, working stitches 4–2, 5–2, 6–2, 7–2, 8–2, and 9–2. The first Star Eyelet is complete.

**4.** Using the *same* thread, work the overlapping Star Stitch as shown on the diagram in solid black and marked with letters of the alphabet (A–B, 2–B, C–B, D–B, E–B, etc.).

## OFFSET RECTANGLE EYELET (FREE EYES).

The sample is worked on 25-count Zweigart® Dublin Linen with DMC® Cotton Floss (1 strand).

This stitch gives you the freedom to create a rectangle of any size with the center hole placed off-center anywhere you choose within the rectangle. The diagram shows only one of the choices.

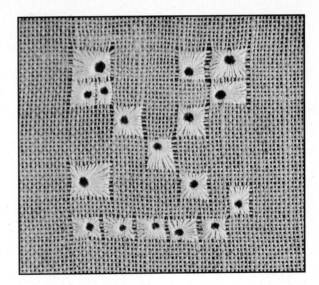

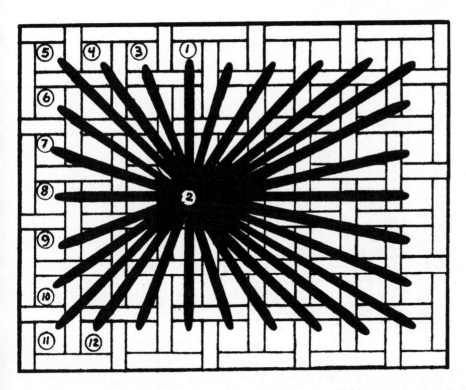

1. Bring the needle up at 1 and down at 2 (over 3 horizontal fabric threads). This space (2) becomes the eyelet hole. All the stitches are worked *into* this hole.

2. Working in a counterclockwise direction, bring the needle up at 3 (under 1 vertical and 3 horizontal fabric threads) and back down at 2. Continue around in this manner, following the diagram numbers, until the rectangle is complete.

# ROUND EYELET.

The sample is worked on 25-count Zweigart®
Lugana with DMC® Cotton Floss (1 strand) or #12
Perle Cotton.

This is a simple Eyelet Stitch that produces a
light, allover pattern. Use a *light to medium pull*.

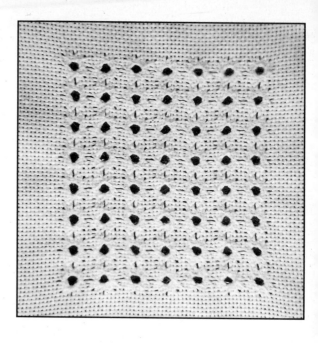

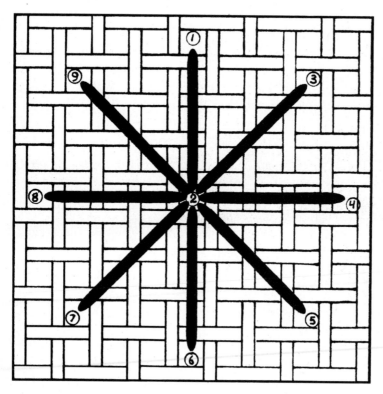

**1.** Bring the needle up at 1 and
down over 4 horizontal fabric
threads into the center hole (2).

**2.** Working in a clockwise direction, bring the needle up at 3
(under 3 horizontal and vertical
fabric threads) and back into the
center hole (2).

**3.** Return to the front at 4 (under 4
vertical fabric threads) and back
down (over 4 vertical fabric
threads) at 2.

**4.** Continue around, following the
numbers on the diagram, until the
round shape is complete (9–2).

*Note: To stitch counterclockwise,
start at 9.*

## SINGLE-CROSS EYELET (LARGE).

The sample is worked on 25-count Zweigart® Lugana with DMC® #8 Perle Cotton.

This is a beautiful Eyelet Stitch worked in four parts (each corner) that produces a single cross in the center. The composite stitches (all four corners) can be worked edge to edge or with a fabric thread separating them. *Work with a medium pull.*

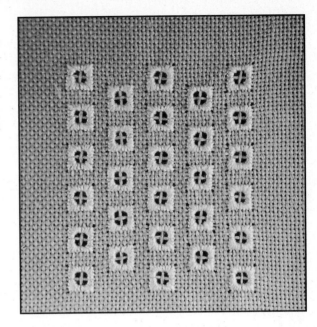

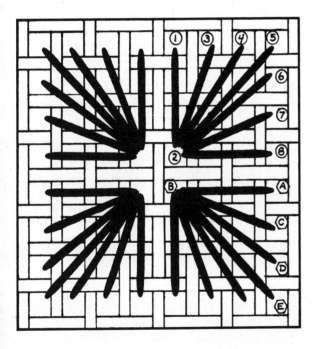

1. Bring the needle up at 1 and down at 2 (over 3 horizontal fabric threads).

2. Bring the needle up at 3 (under 1 vertical and 3 horizontal fabric threads) and back down at 2.

3. Following the diagram, continue around in a clockwise direction until the corner is complete (8–2).

4. To start the next corner, skip 1 horizontal fabric thread and bring the needle up at A and down (over 3 vertical fabric threads) at B. Continue around as for the first corner until this corner is complete.

5. Repeat for each corner.

## SINGLE-CROSS EYELET (SMALL).

The sample is worked on 25-count Zweigart® Lugana with DMC® #12 Perle Cotton.

    This stitch is worked exactly like the large Single-Cross Eyelet. However, because it is worked over 2 fabric threads it produces a more dense pattern. *Use a medium pull.*

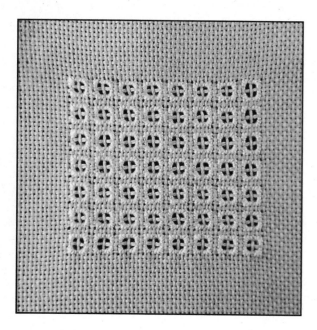
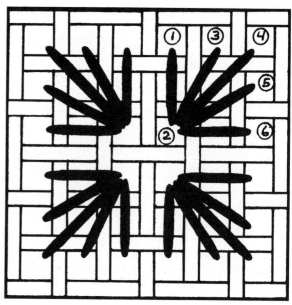

## FAGGOT STITCH (SINGLE FAGGOT)

The sample is worked on 25-count Zweigart® Lugana with DMC® Cotton Floss.

    This stitch is used as a filling by placing rows together to form squares. It requires a tight tension.

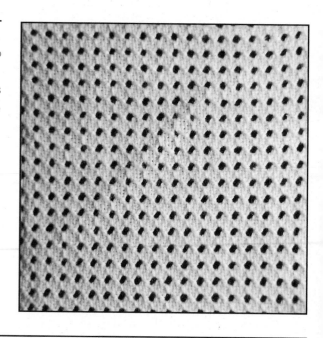

1. Bring the thread up from the back at 1 and down over 4 vertical fabric threads to the right at 2.

2. Bring the needle up at 3 (4 horizontal threads down and 4 vertical threads to the left) and down at 4.

3. Bring the needle up at 5 and down at 6; continue in this pattern to the end of the row.

4. To start a second row, bring the needle to the front four vertical and horizontal threads to the right. Turn the work around to work the second row.

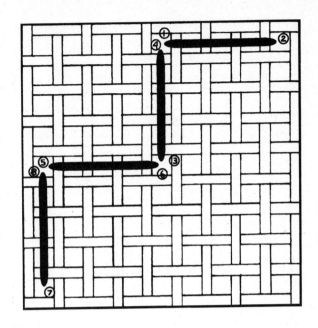

## FAGGOT STITCH, DOUBLE (DOUBLE FAGGOT FILLING)

The sample is worked on 25-count Zweigart® Lugana with DMC® #12 Perle Cotton.

This variation of the Faggot Stitch produces a firm, square textured pattern. Use a firm pull to get the open appearance.

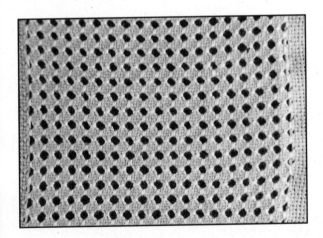

A

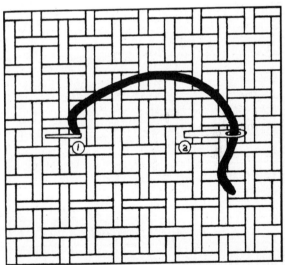

1. Bring the thread through to the front at 1 and down at 2 (4 vertical fabric threads to the right). Bring it back to the front at 1 (in the same space).

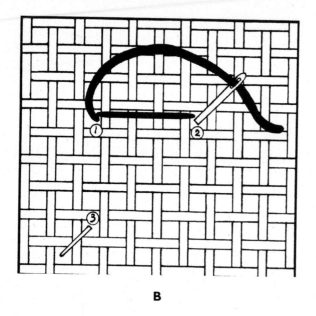

**B**

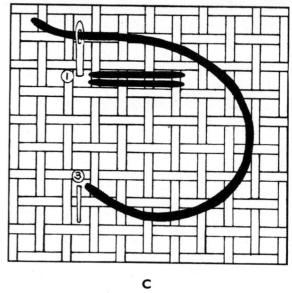

**C**

2. Insert the needle again at 2 and back out at 3 (4 horizontal fabric threads down and 4 vertical fabric threads to the left).

3. Insert the needle back into 1 (4 horizontal fabric threads up) and down again in 3 (4 horizontal fabric threads down).

4. Place the needle back into 1 and bring it back to the front at 4 (4 horizontal fabric threads down and 4 vertical fabric threads to the left).

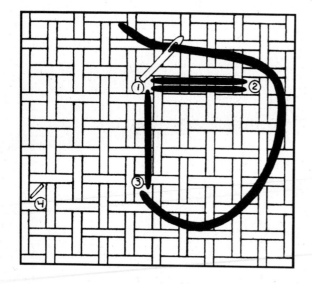

**D**

**5.** Continue in this manner, following the numbers on Diagram E, to the end of the row. To complete the last stitch (5–4), insert the needle in 4 and bring it out to the front at 6.

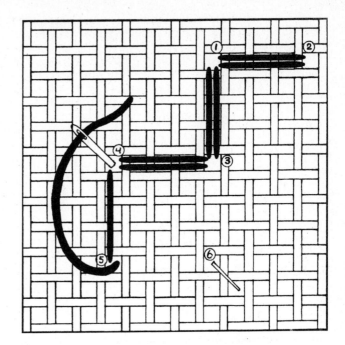

E

**6.** *Turn the work upside-down to work the next row.* Insert the needle at 7 and bring it back to the front at 6. Continue working as for the previous row.

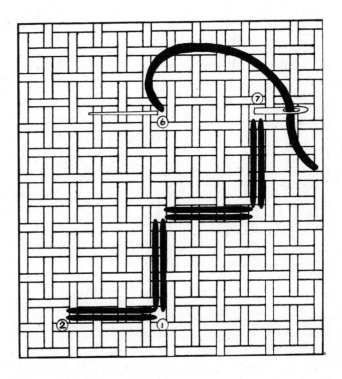

F

# FESTOON #1 (FESTOON STITCH, FESTOON STITCH FILLING)

The sample is worked on 25-count Zweigart® Lugana with DMC® #8 Perle Cotton.

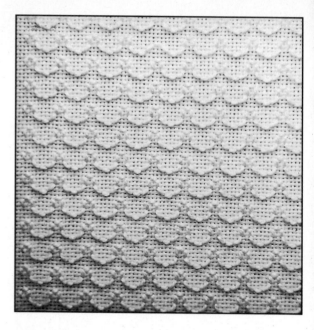

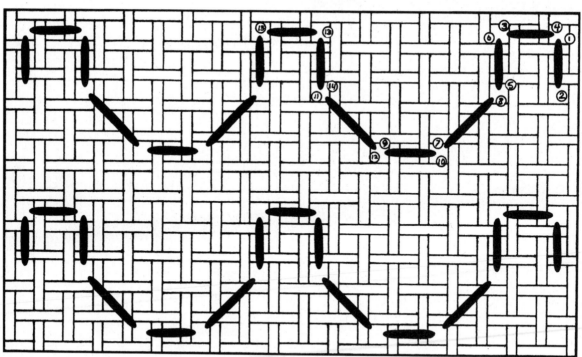

1. Using the diagram, start at 1–2, working Backstitches straight across the row.

2. Work the second and all other rows as shown on the diagram.

## FESTOON #2

The sample is worked on 28-count Zweigart® Brittany with DMC® #12 Perle Cotton.

This is an enlarged version of Festoon #1, worked over 3 instead of 2 fabric threads. To achieve greater definition, work each Backstitch two times in the same holes and pull firmly on the thread.

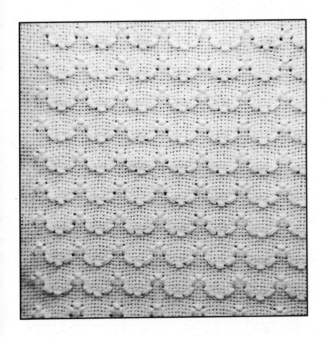

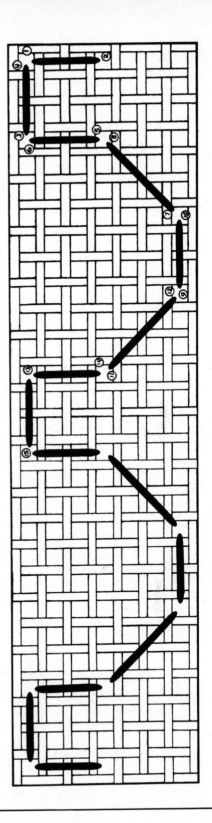

## FINNISH FILLING

The sample is worked on 25-count Zweigart®
Dublin Linen with DMC® #8 Perle Cotton.

This is an allover filling based on the Double
Backstitch (see page 105). It is made of blocks of
Double Backstitches worked in diagonal steps.
Always remember to work over the same number
of fabric threads throughout.

The first row of blocks is shown in the diagram
in solid black. The second row of blocks is shown
in shaded stripes. *Always work from right to left
for each row.*

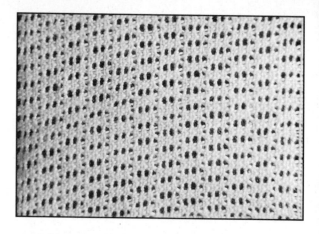

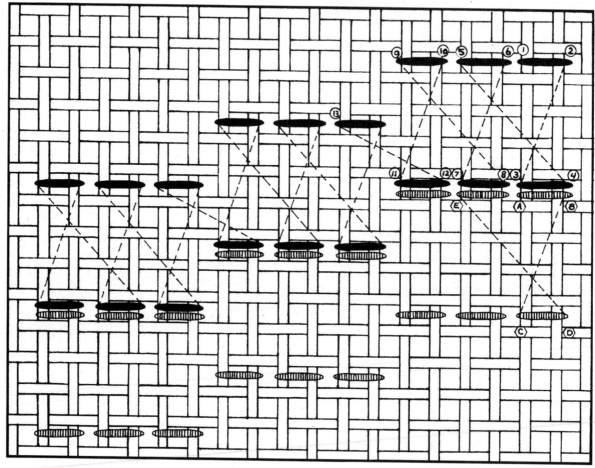

1. Begin at 1–2. Then follow the directions for Double Backstitch on page 105.

2. Begin the second row in the same spaces as 3–4 (A–B). Continue as before across the row.

## GREEK CROSS-STITCH (LACY FILLING, GREEK CROSS SQUARED FILLING)

The sample is worked on 28-count Zweigart® Brittany with DMC® #8 Perle Cotton.

Always work this stitch on stretcher strips or another type of frame. Worked diagonally and staggered, it forms a lacy filling. Worked diagonally with the legs over each other, it forms a squared pattern that is also called Greek Cross Squared Filling.

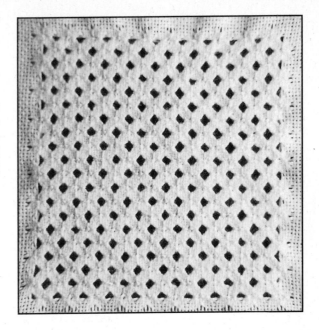

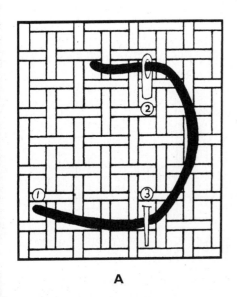

**A**

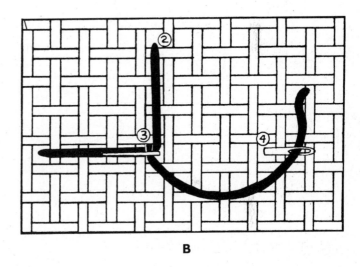

**B**

1. Following Diagram A, bring the thread up at 1 and put the needle in a 2, bringing the needle point through to the front at 3 while keeping the thread under the point of the needle.

2. Pull the needle and thread through and insert the needle back into the fabric at 4 with the tip of the needle coming through to the front at 3 and keeping the thread under the point of the needle.

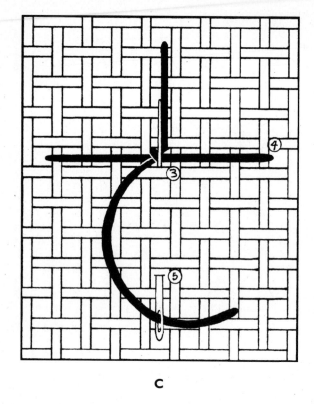
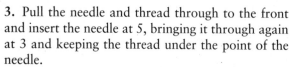
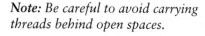

**C**

**3.** Pull the needle and thread through to the front and insert the needle at 5, bringing it through again at 3 and keeping the thread under the point of the needle.

*Note: Be careful to avoid carrying threads behind open spaces.*

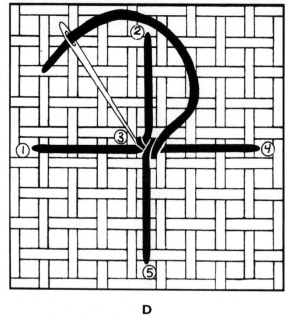

**D**

**4.** Pull the needle and thread through to the front and insert the needle again at 3, crossing the last and first stitches. The last diagram (E) shows the completed Greek Cross-Stitch.

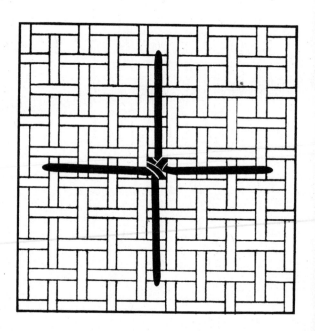

**E**

## HOLBEIN (DOUBLE RUNNING STITCH)

The sample is worked on Zweigart® Aida #14 with DMC® Cotton Floss.

This is the basic outline stitch for Blackwork and Pulled Thread.

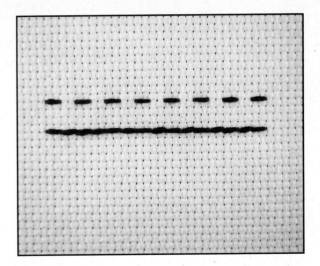

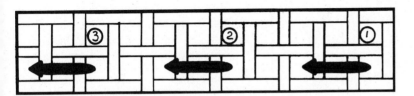

1. Bring the thread up from the back at 1 and down over 2 vertical fabric threads.

2. Bring the needle up under 2 vertical fabric threads and down over 2 vertical fabric threads. Continue across the row.

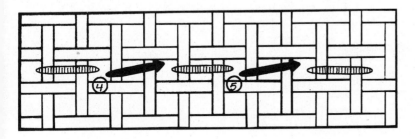

3. For the return trip, bring the needle up at 4 and down over 2 vertical fabric threads (filling in the spaces and forming a straight line or outline). Continue to end of row.

*Note: On the return trip, notice that the stitches in shared holes are worked on a slight angle, coming up from the back under the stitch already worked and going in over the next stitch already worked.*

# HONEYCOMB FILLING

The sample is worked on 25-count Zweigart® Dublin Linen with DMC® #8 Perle Cotton.

This stitch may be worked over 2, 3, or 4 fabric threads, producing a more dense or more open lacy appearance. All the stitches used are Backstitches (see page 94) and are worked with a *firm* tension.

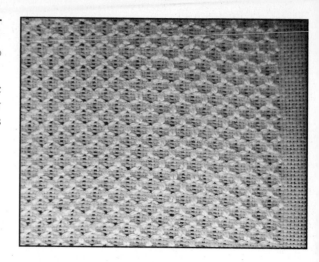

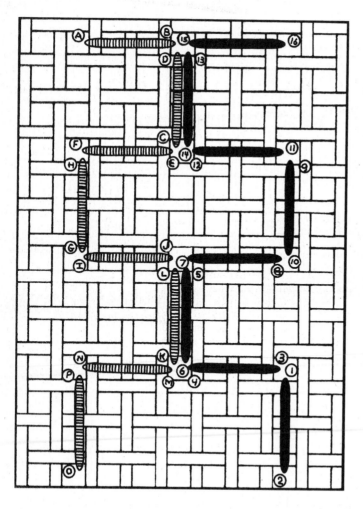

1. Start at 1–2. Follow the numbers in the diagram to the end of the row. These first-row stitches are shown on the diagram in solid black and are marked with numbers.

2. The return trip is shown on the diagram as striped stitches using letters of the alphabet.

3. Repeat these 2 rows, always working *into* the same holes as the previous row.

## MOSAIC FILLING STITCH
### (MOSAIC FILLING, MOSAIC STITCH FILLING)

The sample is worked on 25-count Zweigart®
Lugana with DMC® #8 Perle Cotton.
*Work with a firm tension.*

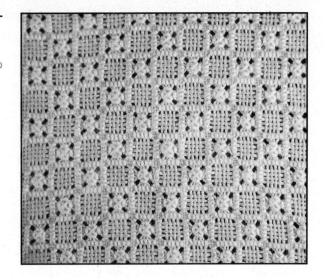

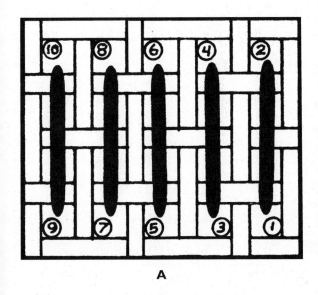

**A**

1. Start at 1, working 5 Satin Stitches (see page 51)
over 3 fabric threads to form a block.

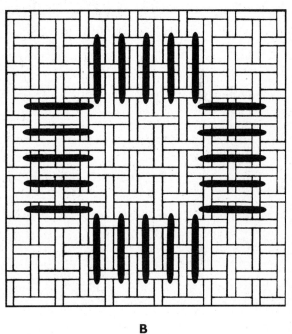

**B**

2. Turn the fabric ¼ turn to the right and work
another block. Work a total of 4 blocks to form a
square, as shown in Diagram B.

**3.** Next, work a Square Stitch (see page 146), following the letters A–B, C–D, E–F, G–H, as shown in Diagram C.

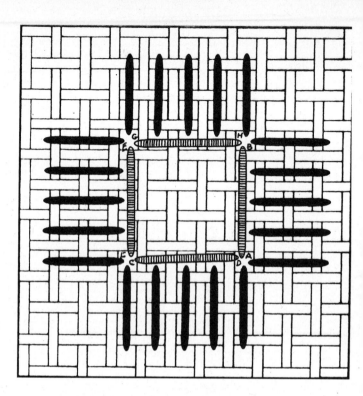

C

**4.** Form a Cross-Stitch (see page 45) in the center of the square, following the letters I–J, K–L, as shown in diagram D.

*Note: For this sample, the Mosaic Filling blocks are staggered in a checkerboard pattern, leaving 4 fabric threads between each block.*

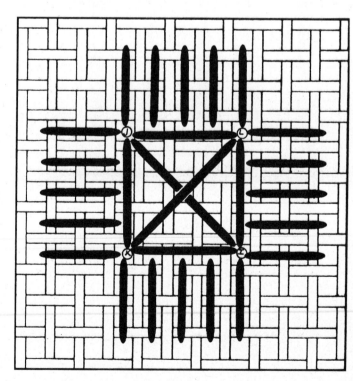

D

## NET FILLING

The sample is worked on 25-count Zweigart® Lugana with DMC® #8 Perle Cotton.

This is a lacy filling stitch worked with a firm pull. It is a combination of large and small Faggot Stitches (see page 120) worked in diagonal rows.

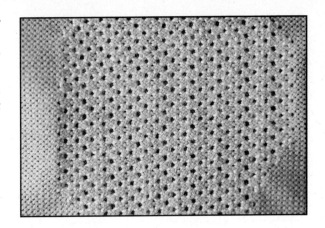

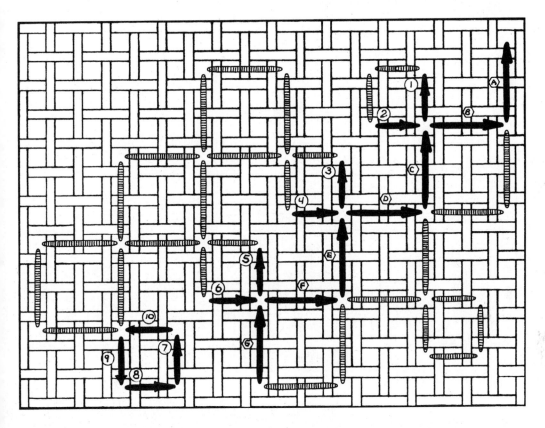

1. Following the directions of the arrows on the diagram, start by working the shorter stitches over 2 fabric threads (1, 2, 3, 4, 5, 6, etc.).

2. Next, following the diagram and the directions of the arrows, work the longer stitches over 3 fabric threads. These are marked on the diagram with A, B, C, D, etc.

3. Continue in this manner (as shown in shaded stitches on the diagram) until the area is filled.

## OPEN BASKET (BASKETWEAVE)

The sample is worked on 25-count Zweigart® Brittany with DMC® #8 Perle Cotton.

This is another Satin Stitch filling that creates a basketlike effect. Work with a *tight, firm* tension.

**1.** Following the diagram, work vertical groups of Satin Stitches over 3 horizontal fabric threads (1–2, 3–4, 5–6, etc.).

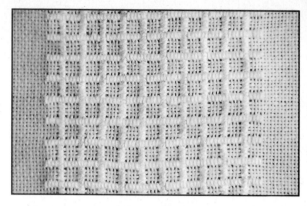

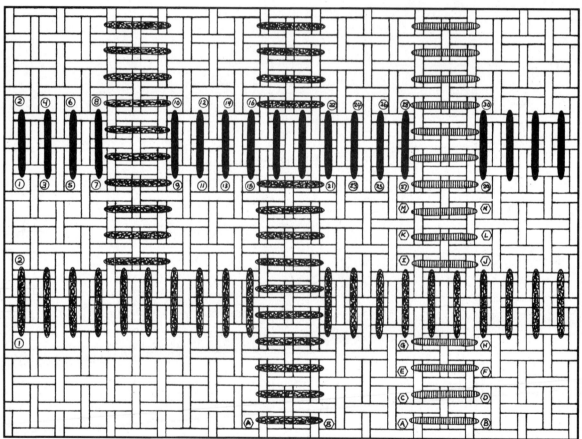

*Note: The diagram shows 10 central stitches with 4 compensating stitches at beginning and end.*

**2.** Next, work the horizontal rows of Satin Stitches over 3 vertical fabric threads.

*Note: Be careful to follow the diagram exactly to achieve the basketweave look.*

## OUTLINED DIAMOND EYELET

The sample is worked on 25-count Zweigart®
Lugana with DMC® Cotton Floss.

This filling stitch is composed of Diamond Eyelets that are worked over an even number of vertical and horizontal fabric threads, and Diagonal Satin Stitches forming an outline around them. In this sample, the Eyelet Stitch is worked over 10 horizontal and 10 vertical fabric threads. The Satin Stitches are worked over 2 vertical and 2 horizontal fabric threads.

*Note: Use a firm pull or tension for this stitch.*

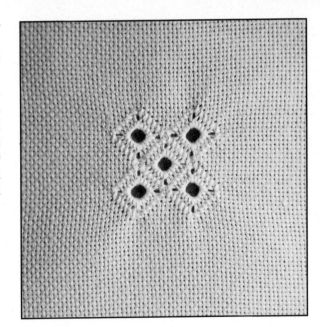

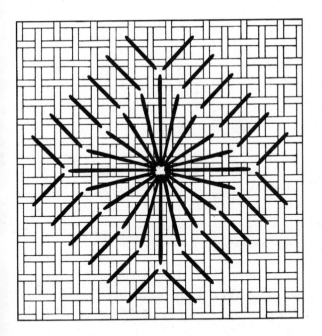

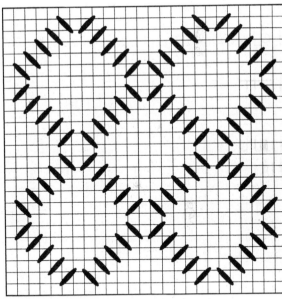

1. Work the Diagonal Satin Stitches (see variation 2 on page 53).

2. Then fill the formed centers with the Diamond Eyelets (see page 111).

## PEBBLE STITCH FILLING

The sample is worked on 25-count Zweigart® Lugana with DMC® #8 Perle Cotton.

This is an easy-to-learn stitch that is worked in horizontal rows. Use a *firm pull* throughout.

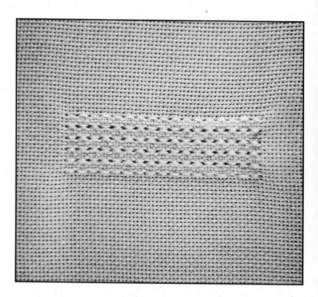

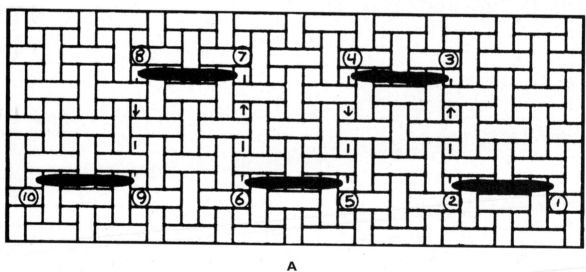

**A**

**1.** Come up at 1 and down at 2 (over 3 vertical fabric threads).

**2.** Go up under three horizontal fabric threads, coming up at 3, and down at 4 (over 3 vertical fabric threads). Continue across the row as shown in Diagram A.

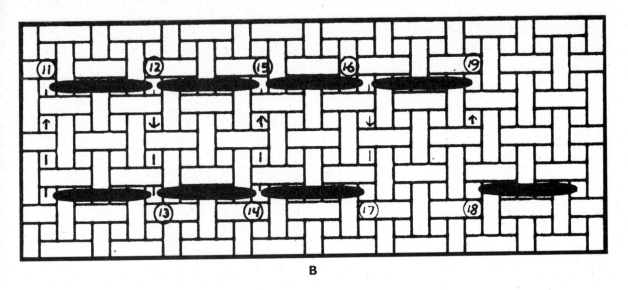

B

3. This is the return trip. Come up to the top of the row at 11 and go down at 12 (space 12 is the same as space 8 in Diagram A). Following the numbers in Diagram B, fill in the missing stitches.

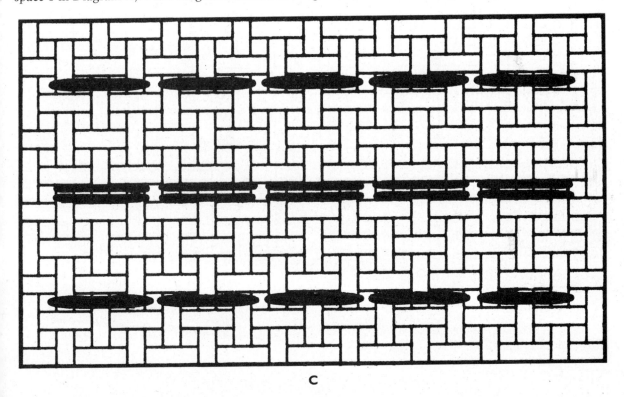

C

4. Repeat steps 1 to 3 for each row. Note that the second and all future rows share the holes of the previous row.

## RINGED BACKSTITCH (BACKSTITCH, RINGED, RINGED BACK)

The sample is worked on 25-count Zweigart® Dublin Linen with DMC® #8 Perle Cotton.

You can work this stitch in rows to form a border or blocked one above the other to make an allover filling pattern.

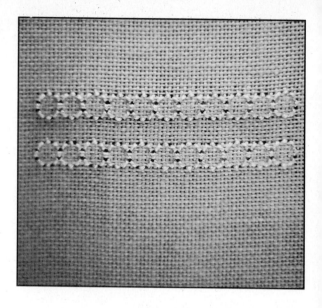

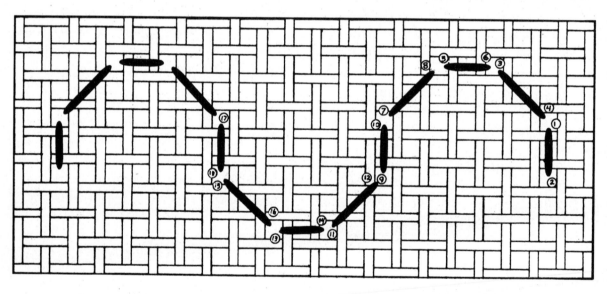

**A**

**1.** Using a firm pull, this stitch is worked entirely in Backstitches, forming a pattern that produces half-rings (see Diagram A).

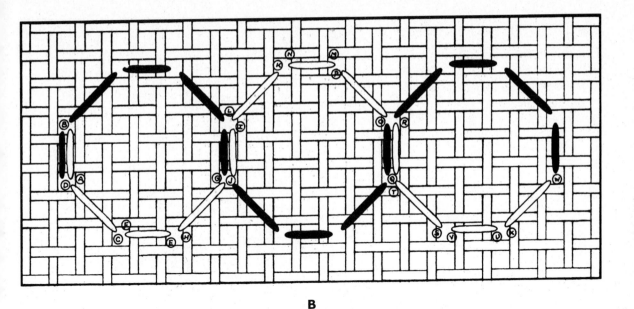

**B**

**2.** The return trip, shown in white on Diagram B, completes the other half-rings, resulting in a Ringed Backstitch.

*Note: All connecting stitches between the rings are worked into the same holes.*

## RUNNING STITCH

The sample is worked on Zweigart® Aida #14 with DMC® Cotton Floss.

This is the basic stitch used in Pattern Darning and the first part of the Holbein Stitch (see pages 83 and 129) that is used for Blackwork and Assisi outlining (see pages 17 and 13).

*Note: This stitch can be worked over or under 2 or more fabric threads.*

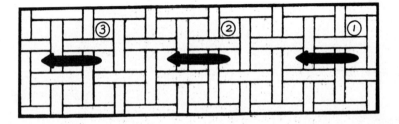

**1.** Bring the thread up from the back at 1 and down over 2 vertical fabric threads to the left.

**2.** Bring the needle up under 2 vertical fabric threads and down over 2 vertical fabric threads.

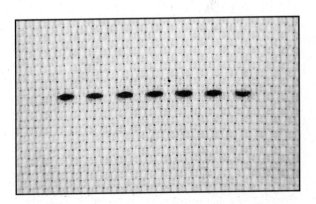

# RUNNING STITCH FILLING

The sample is worked on Zweigart® 25-count Dublin Linen with DMC® #8 Perle Cotton.

This easy filling stitch produces a light, wavy effect when pulled with a firm tension. Notice that the flat lines on the diagrams give a diagonal effect when stitched and pulled on the sample.

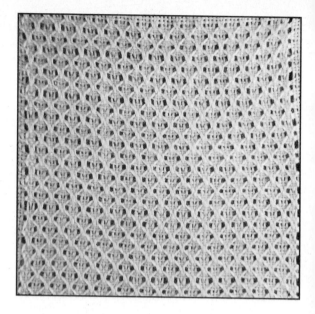

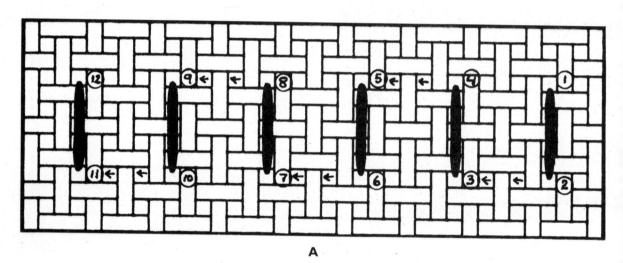

**A**

1. Bring the thread through to the front at 1 and down to the back at 2.

2. Following the directions of the arrows and the numbers, continue across the row.

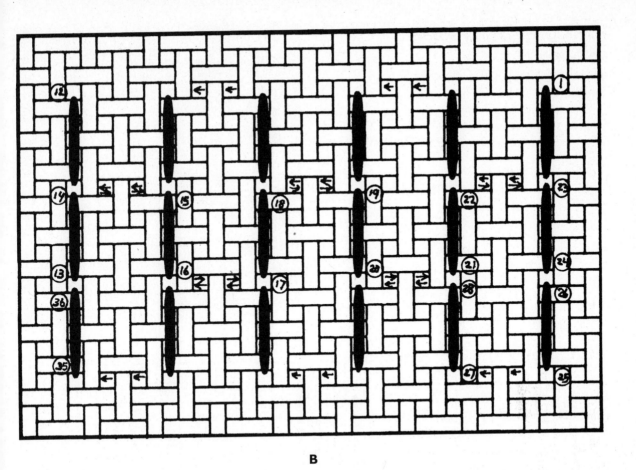

**B**

3. To start Row 2, put the needle down under 6 horizontal fabric threads, bringing it to the front at 13. Continue to follow diagram (B) to the end of the row. Notice that the threads of Row 2 share the bottom holes of Row 1.

4. Continue in this way until the area to be stitched is filled.

## SATIN STITCH DIAMONDS
(SATIN DIAMOND BLOCKS)

The sample is worked on 25-count Zweigart®
Lugana with DMC® #8 Perle Cotton.

This stitch can be worked with no pull or tension
to give the appearance of a Satin Diamond pattern
or pulled with a firm tension for a lacy look.

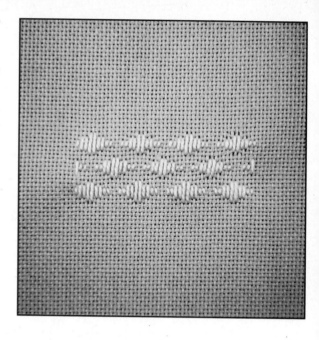

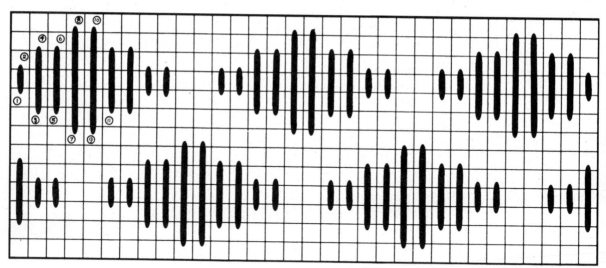

1. Following the diagram, work the stitches across each row.

2. If using a firm pull or tension, end off each row and start the next row at the left side.

## SMALL CHESSBOARD FILLING

The sample is worked on 25-count Zweigart®
Lugana with DMC® #8 Perle Cotton.

This is one of the Satin Stitch filling stitches that
is used for a dainty effect when pulled tightly.

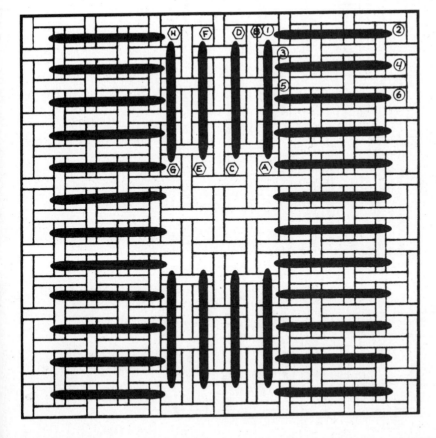

1. Following the diagram,
work the vertical rows of horizontal Satin Stitches over 4
vertical fabric threads (1–2,
3–4, 5–6, etc.).

2. Next, work the 4 vertical
Satin Stitches between the
rows (A–B, C–D, E–F, G–H).

3. Continue until the desired
area is filled.

## SPACED SATIN FILLING

The sample is worked on 32-count Zweigart® Belfast Linen with DMC® #12 Perle Cotton.

This stitch is made of blocks of Satin Stitches evenly spaced across the area to be worked. It requires a *firm* pull or tension to achieve the lacy, open look.

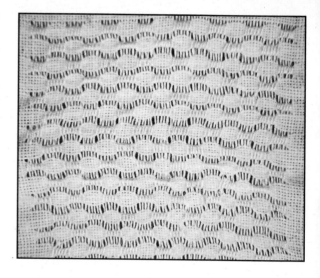

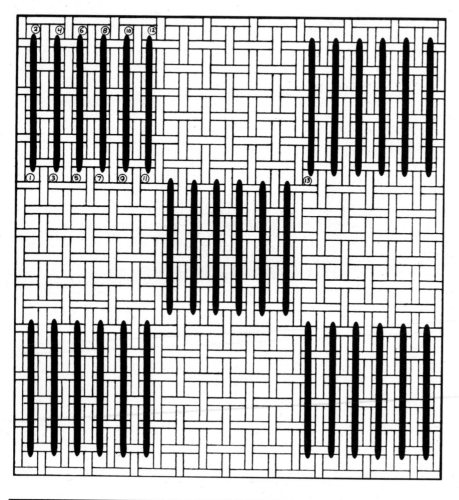

**1.** Work 6 Satin Stitches (page 51) over 6 horizontal fabric threads to form the first block.

**2.** Continue across the row as shown in the diagram.

**3.** The next row of Satin Stitch blocks is placed *between* the blocks of the first row.

## STAR STITCH (STAR EYELET)

The sample is worked on 25-count Zweigart® Lugana with DMC® #8 Cotton Floss.

This stitch is worked over an even number of vertical and horizontal fabric threads and forms a square. The sample is worked over 6 threads *with almost no tension.*

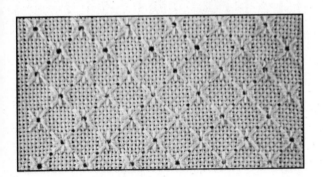

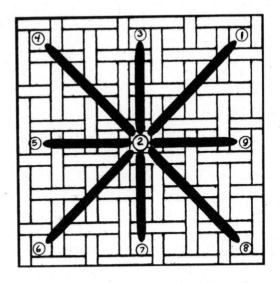

1. Bring the thread through to the front at 1 and down at 2 (3 horizontal fabric threads down and 3 vertical fabric threads to the left).

2. Bring the needle up at 3 (3 horizontal fabric threads up) and back down at 2.

3. Continue working counterclockwise according to the diagram.

*Note: This stitch can be worked over any even number of vertical and horizontal fabric threads (6, 8, 12, etc.).*

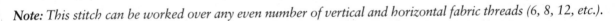

## STAR STITCH (SMALL)

The sample is worked on 25-count Zweigart® Dublin Linen with DMC® Cotton Floss.

This stitch is worked over an equal number of vertical and horizontal fabric threads. The sample is worked over 4 fabric threads. *Do not pull tightly.*

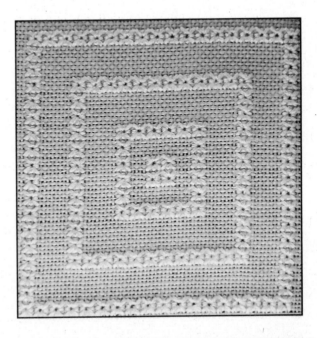

1. Bring the needle through to the front at 1 and down at 2 (2 fabric threads down and 2 to the left).

2. Bring the needle up at 3 (2 horizontal fabric threads up) and back down into 2.

3. Continue working counterclockwise according to the diagram.

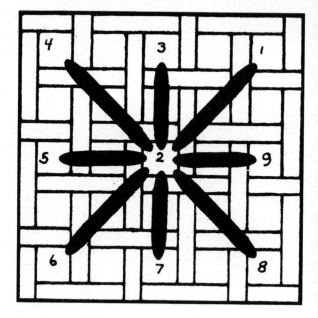

*Note: This stitch can be worked in rows (edge to edge) as a border, staggered, or as a filling.*

## SQUARE STITCH #1 (FLAT SQUARE STITCH, 4-SIDED STITCH)

The sample is worked on 28-count Zweigart® Brittany with DMC® #12 Perle Cotton.

This is one of the most popular Pulled-Thread stitches. It is used mainly for borders and uses a *medium pull*.

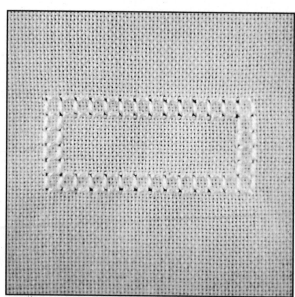

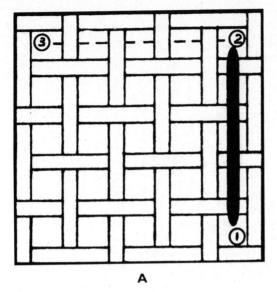

A

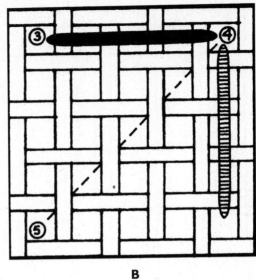

B

**1.** Come up from the back at 1 and down at 2 (over 4 horizontal fabric threads).

**2.** Return to the front at 3 (under 4 vertical fabric threads to the left) and go down at 4 (over 4 vertical fabric threads to the right). Return to the front at 5 (diagonally under 4 vertical and 4 horizontal fabric threads).

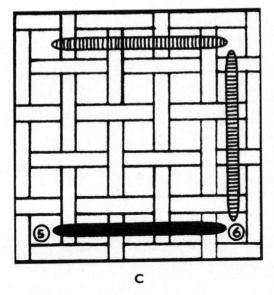

C

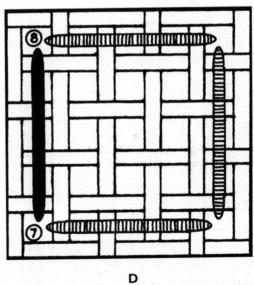

D

**3.** Go down at 6 (over 4 vertical fabric threads to the right).

**4.** Come back up at 5 (now called 7) and go back down at 8 (over 4 horizontal fabric threads).

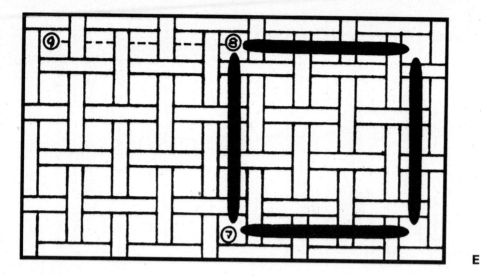

E

5. To start the next square, return to the front at 9 (under 4 vertical fabric threads to the left).

6. Continue working across the row, creating squares.

## SQUARE STITCH #2 (RAISED SQUARE STITCH)

The sample is worked on 28-count Zweigart® Brittany with DMC® #12 Perle Cotton.

This is another Square Stitch and probably one of the most popular Pulled-Thread stitches. Follow the numbering on the diagrams to achieve the raised, textural look *This stitch requires a very firm pull.*

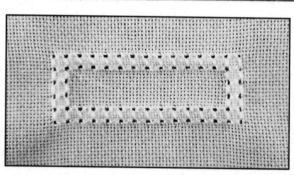

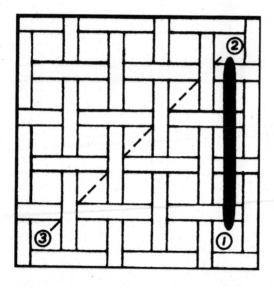

A

1. Come up from the back at 1 and down at 2 (over 4 horizontal fabric threads).

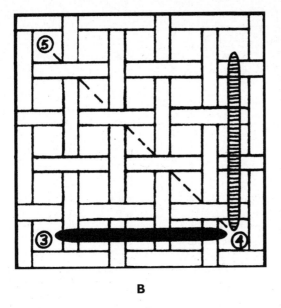

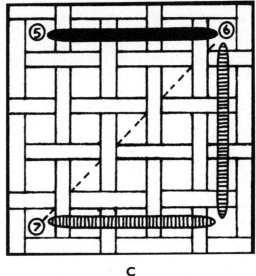

**B**

**C**

**2.** Return to the front at 3 (diagonally under 4 vertical and 4 horizontal fabric threads) and down at 4 (over 4 vertical fabric threads).

**3.** Come back to the front at 5 (under 4 vertical and 4 horizontal fabric threads) and down at 6 (over 4 vertical fabric threads). Return to the front at 7 (under 4 vertical and 4 horizontal fabric threads). *The cross formed on the wrong side of the fabric creates the raised stitch.*

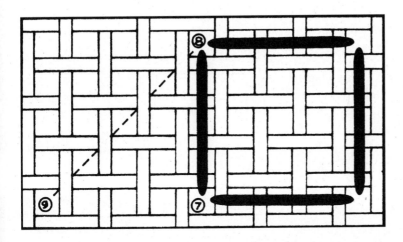

**D**

**4.** Go down at 8 (over 4 horizontal fabric threads) and return to the front at 9 (diagonally under 4 horizontal and 4 vertical fabric threads).

**5.** Continue making raised squares across the row.

*Note: Stitch 7–8 equals stitch 1–2 of the next square. To work a second row, turn the fabric and work the stitches in the same manner. Work the connecting stitches into the same holes as those of the previous row.*

# SQUARE STITCH #3 (DIAGONAL RAISED SQUARE STITCH)

The sample is worked on 28-count Zweigart® Brittany with DMC® #12 Perle Cotton.

This is basically the same stitch as the Square Stitch #2 (Raised Square Stitch), except that it is worked on the diagonal. To work as a filling, stagger the rows.

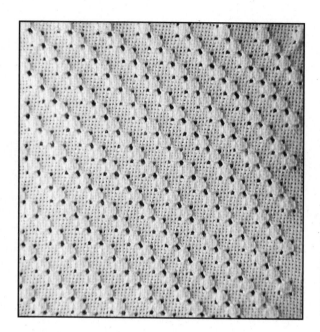 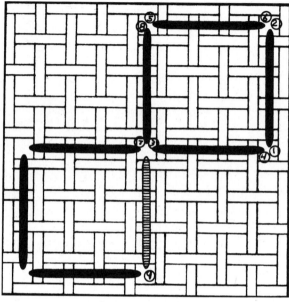

**1.** Bring the needle to the front at 1 and down at 2 (over 4 horizontal fabric threads).

**2.** Come to the front at 3 (diagonally under 4 vertical and 4 horizontal fabric threads) and down at 4 (over 4 vertical fabric threads).

**3.** Return to the front at 5 (diagonally under 4 vertical and 4 horizontal fabric threads) and down at 6. *The cross that creates the raised stitch is now formed.*

**4.** Bring the needle to the front at 7 (under 4 horizontal and 4 vertical fabric threads) and down at 8 (over 4 horizontal fabric threads).

**5.** To begin the second square, bring the needle back to the front at 9 (under 8 horizontal fabric threads). Continue as with the first square.

# WINDOW STITCH

The sample is worked on 25-count Zweigart® Dublin Linen with DMC® #8 Perle Cotton.

This stitch gives a lacy appearance and requires a firm tension.

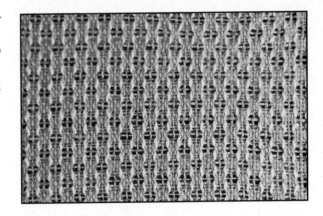

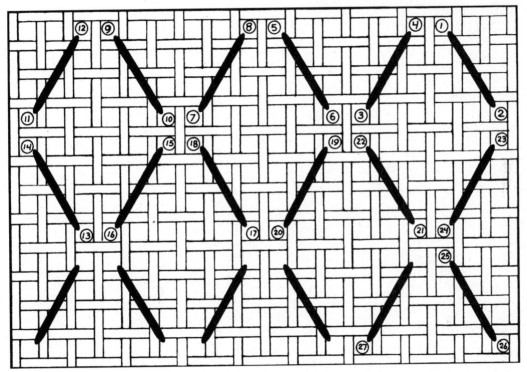

1. Bring the needle up from the back at 1 and down at 2 (over 3 horizontal and 2 vertical fabric threads).

2. Bring the needle back up to the front at 3 (under 5 vertical fabric threads to the left) and down again at 4 (over 3 horizontal threads up and 2 vertical fabric threads to the right.)3. Bring the needle back up to the front at 5 (under 5 vertical fabric threads to the left) and down at 6 (over 3 horizontal threads down and 2 vertical fabric threads to the right).

4. Continue across the row, following the diagram.

5. To start the second row, turn the work around, bringing the needle to the front at 13. Always work this stitch from right to left.

# Projects

## ASSISI EMBROIDERY BOOKMARK

This sample was started by Marilyn Goldberg. When her illness prevented her from completing the book-mark, she asked me to have it completed by someone so that it could be included in my book. Jacqui O'Connell finished it to help me honor one of Marilyn's last requests.

## MATERIALS

Zweigart® Aida #14 (6″ × 12″)

DMC® Floss #310 Black (1 skein) and #666 Red (1 skein)

#24 tapestry needle

Stretcher bars and thumbtacks (6″ × 12″)

Backing fabric (2½″ × 8″)

## PREPARATION

**1.** Attach Aida fabric to stretcher bars with thumbtacks.

**2.** Mark center lines (horizontal and vertical) with a basting thread.

**3.** Copy your chosen initials and year onto chart from Assisi alphabet (page 180).

## TO WORK

**1.** Following the diagram, with 1 strand DMC® Floss #310, work the outline around the entire pattern using the Holbein Stitch (see page 129) or Backstitch (see page 94).

**2.** Fill in background Cross-Stitches as shown on the diagram.

**3.** Trim fabric to within ½″ of embroidery. Fold to back and press.

**4.** Trim backing to same size (plus ¼″) on all sides. Press edges under to back and attach with an iron-on fabric or slip-stitch the edges together.

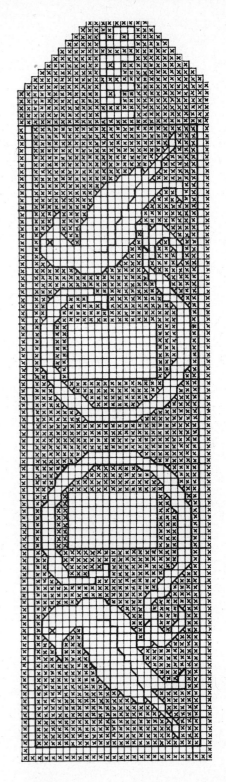

# ASSISI EMBROIDERY BORDER TOWEL

Assisi patterns work very well on manufactured soft goods with an Aida band insert. The Charles Craft towel used here has a #14 Aida band insert with 32 fabric threads.

## MATERIALS

Charles Craft towel with #14 Aida insert

DMC® Floss #666 (1 skein)

DMC® #5 Perle Cotton

#24 tapestry needle

Assisi alphabet chart (see "Alphabets," page 180)

## PREPARATION

**1.** Photocopy the Assisi alphabet chart. Paste your chosen initials (or copy with pencil) in the rectangular spaces left open on the diagram.

**2.** Baste center line on fabric band.

## TO WORK

**1.** Using #5 Black Perle Cotton, following the diagram, work Holbein Stitch (page 129) or Backstitch (page 94), outlining the pattern. *Do not forget to outline each initial.*

**2.** Work Cross-Stitches to fill in the background. Remember to work Cross-Stitches around the initials. *Leave white areas unworked.*

**3.** Continue working Cross-Stitches to within 2 to 3 fabric threads on top, bottom, and sides of band insert.

*Note: The Bookmark photograph shows the same pattern with initials inserted.*

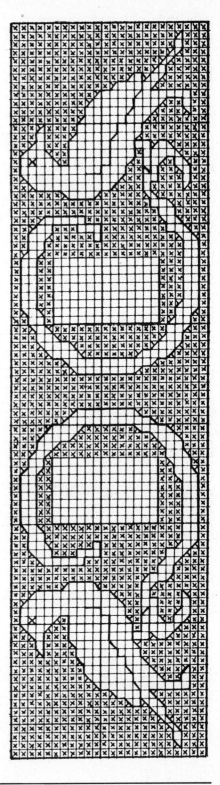

# ASSISI EMBROIDERY ALPHABET SAMPLER

This alphabet can be framed as a sampler or used in some of the projects where noted in the instructions.

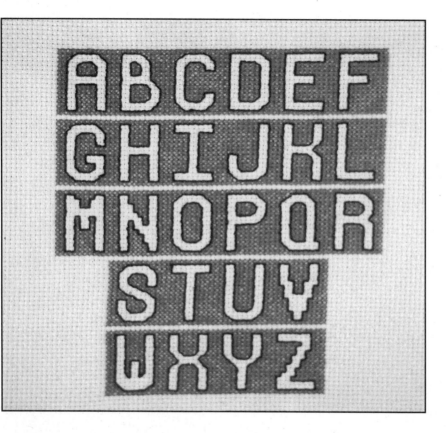

## MATERIALS

Zweigart® Aida #14 (9″ × 10″)

DMC® Perle Cotton #8 (1 spool)

DMC® Floss #666 (1 skein)

#24 tapestry needle

Stretcher bars (9″ × 10″)

## PREPARATION

1. Put fabric on stretcher bars with thumbtacks.
2. Mark center of fabric with basting thread.

## TO WORK

**1.** Following the diagram, use #8 Perle Cotton and outline the letters in Backstitch (page 94) or Holbein Stitch (page 129).

**2.** Fill in the background around the letters with Cross-Stitches over 1 fabric thread with 2 or 3 strands of DMC® Floss #666.

**3.** To use as a sampler, I suggest filling in the background completely (omitting the white spaces between the lines of the letters and stitching to the edges on S-T-U-V and W-X-Y-Z.

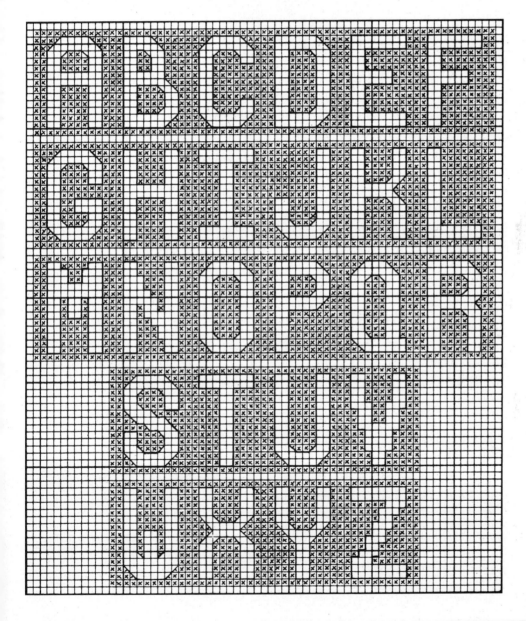

# ASSISI ELEPHANT BORDER BREAD COVER

## MATERIALS

Charles Craft Bread Cover with Aida #14 insert (18" × 18")

DMC® Floss #666 (1 skein)

DMC® Floss #310 (1 skein)

#24 tapestry needle

## TO WORK

1. In the first corner, using 2 or 3 strands of Floss #666, work 2 rows of 101 Cross-Stitches, starting 10 fabric threads from each corner edge. If you want to work the border longer or shorter, follow the diagram to count the number of stitches needed for each elephant repeat.

2. Following the diagram, continue working your Cross-Stitches, leaving the elephants *unworked*.

**3.** Using 1 strand of Floss #310, work the outline of the elephants (including the eyes and ears) with Backstitch or Holbein Stitch.

**4.** Repeat for the other side of the corner, following the diagram.

*Note: Always make each side of the same corner the same length.*

**5.** Outline (with Backstitch or Holbein Stitch) the entire corner of Cross-Stitches with 1 strand of Floss #310. Leave 1 fabric thread unworked and work another outline all around.

**6.** Repeat in the *opposite* corner. For the sample only 2 corner elephants were worked. Use the same method as steps 2 to 5.

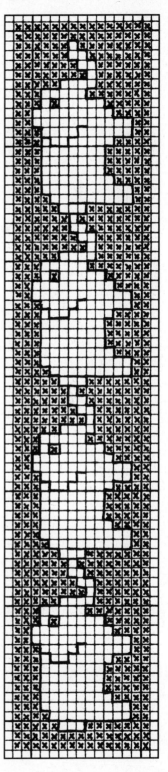

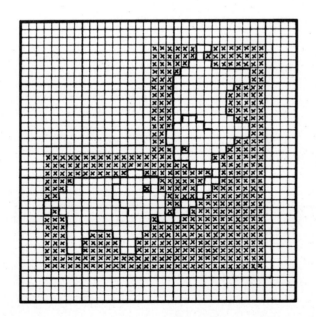

# DALE'S PULLED-THREAD EYEGLASS CASE

This eyeglass case was generously designed and stitched by Dale Sokolow. Her directions are very detailed and exacting and will produce a perfect project is you follow them carefully.

## MATERIALS

Zweigart® 28-count Cashel Linen (10″ × 10″)

DMC® #12 Perle Cotton #3042 (1 spool)

DMC® Floss #3041 (1 skein)

Darice glass seed beads #1106-02 (purple)

Needles: #24 tapestry, #8 and #9 crewel, or a beading needle

Purple interlining (8″ × 8″)

Lining to match fabric (8″ × 8″)

Stretcher bars and thumbtacks (10″ × 10″, or a 6″ hoop—see page 3)

## PREPARATION

**1.** Overcast all edges of the fabric and attach to the stretcher bars with the thumbtacks.

**2.** Start basting the shape of the eyeglass case 1¾″ from the top and 1¾″ from the side. Baste 185 threads across the top and bottom, with 85 threads on the left side and 95 threads on the right side. (Pulled-Thread embroidery will "shrink" the fabric, so more fabric is required to have the front and the back of the eyeglass case the same size.)

## TO WORK

### RINGED BACKSTITCH:

**1.** Start stitching on the right side of the right panel using #12 Perle Cotton and a #24 tapestry needle. *Use a firm pull.*

**2.** The first stitch is located 13 fabric threads down and 12 fabric threads from the right edge. Follow the chart for Ringed Backstitch (see page 138), noting that you will be working the top of 1 circle and then the bottom of the next. At the end of the row (12 circles) reverse direction as shown in the diagram to complete the circles.

**3.** End the thread with a #8 crewel needle by weaving the thread under the pattern on the back and piercing the Perle Cotton thread.

### STEP STITCH VARIATION WITH EYELET:

**1.** This Step Stitch variation consists of 5 stitches over 4 fabric threads each. There are 8 units across and 3 units down.

**2.** Start on the left side using #12 Perle Cotton. *Use a firm pull.*

**3.** The bottom of the first stitch is 10 fabric threads down and 6 fabric threads to the right of the previous row. Work 7 steps down and then reverse direction and work your way up on the right side. Work the remaining area in the same manner.

**4.** When you get to the bottom of the second row, you will have to make a compensation unit to the left. Run your needle through the previously worked stitches to continue the progression.

**5.** The eyelets are worked in the center of each unit. Use 1 strand of DMC® Floss #3401 and the tapestry needle. Come up in the center of each unit and work toward the outside. *Use a firm pull.* (See "Eyelet Stitches, Square Eyelet," page 108). Work the eyelets from the top left unit down to the bottom right unit. Be careful that your carrying thread does not show through from the back.

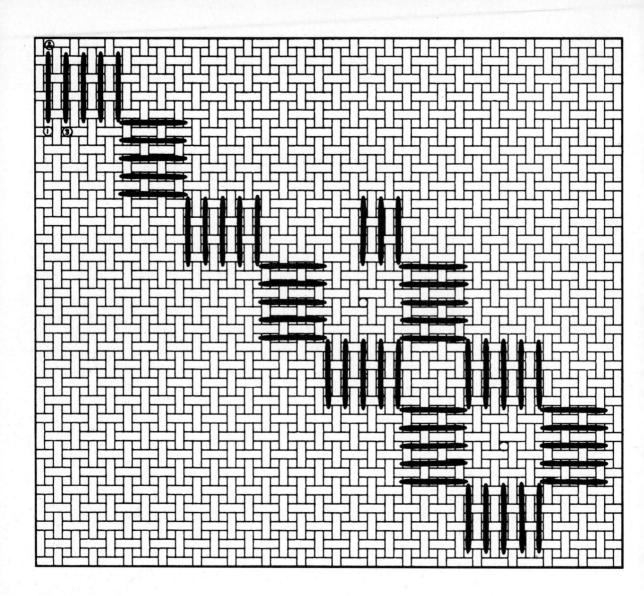

## RINGED BACKSTITCH:

**1.** Start 8 fabric threads down and 2 fabric threads to the right of the pattern above.

**2.** Follow directions for Ringed Backstitch on page 138.

## FINISH FILLING:

**1.** This stitch will be worked sideways, so turn your stretcher bars 90 degrees.

**2.** Use the #12 Perle Cotton and start stitching 8 fabric threads below the last pattern above and 12 fabric threads from the center basting.

**3.** To keep the pulling tight, take a tacking stitch beneath the last stitch of each row. Note that individual stitches in the next row go in the opposite direction.

**4.** Threads are ended by running your needle back and forth behind the units.

**5.** The first and last rows of this pattern have compensation stitches with only 2 fabric threads (rather than 6) between the stitches.

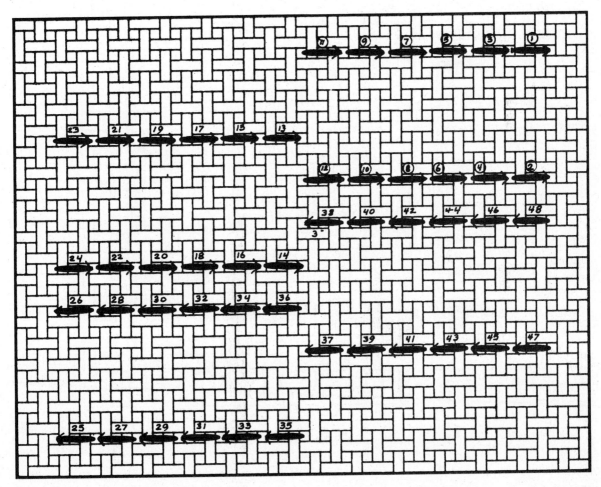

## RINGED BACKSTITCH:

**1.** Start stitching 8 fabric threads down and 1 fabric thread to the right of the previous pattern.

**2.** Follow directions for Ringed Backstitch on page 138.

## CHECKERBOARD:

This unit consists of 3 rows of 10 stitches, each stitch over 3 fabric threads. The next unit is the same, except that it is worked in the opposite direction. This stitch is very similar to Chessboard Filling (see page 96).

**1.** This pattern starts on the right side. Using #12 Perle Cotton and a *firm* pull, start the first stitch 9 fabric threads below and directly below the right side of the pattern above.

**2.** Take a tacking stitch at the end of each unit. Work the units horizontally across the row.

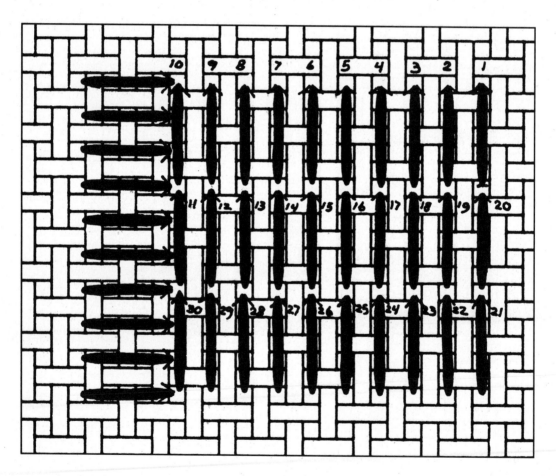

RINGED BACKSTITCH:

1. Start 8 threads down and directly under the previous pattern.

2. Follow directions for Ringed Backstitch on page 138.

## ADDING BEADS

There is a bead in the center of each Ringed Backstitch circle.

Using 1 strand of DMC Floss #3041 in the #9 crewel needle (or a beading needle), attach each bead by coming through the fabric and bead 2 times. Make sure that the traveling thread does not show through the holes.

## FINISHING

1. Attach the interlining to the embroidery by stitching together on the basting line. Have the front of the lining facing the back of the embroidery.

2. Remove the basting thread and trim the interlining to ½".

3. Sew the lining front to the embroidery front along the previous stitching. Work only the top and both sides.

4. Trim the excess fabric and miter the corners.

5. Turn right side out and press carefully, avoiding the beads.

6. Fold in half and sew bottom of lining together.

7. Sew bottom and side of eyeglass case together, to within 1" of the top edge, by overcasting the front and back. Use DMC® Ecru Floss or sewing thread.

# DARNING PATTERN BORDER TOWEL

Darning patterns work up beautifully with or without initials on manufactured soft goods with an Aida band insert. The Charles Craft towel used here has an Aida insert with 32 fabric threads.

## MATERIALS

Charles Craft towel with #14 Aida insert

DMC® Floss #969 (1 skein)

DMC® Floss #970 (18")

#24 tapestry needle

Darning pattern alphabet (page 186)

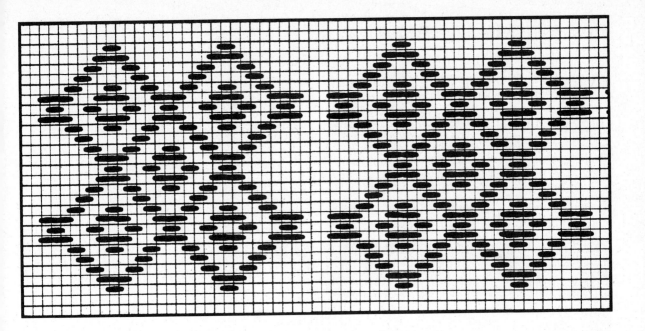

## PREPARATION

1. Copy, or paste from photocopy of the alphabet, your chosen initial(s).

2. Baste center line on fabric band.

## TO WORK

1. Using 3 or 4 strands of DMC® Floss #969, follow the diagram, working in horizontal rows.

2. Using 3 strands of DMC® Floss #970, Cross-Stitch your chosen initial(s) or name.

# EMILY ROSE SAMPLER

The sampler is the prime example of the earliest educational tool of Colonial times, when mothers used it to teach reading and arithmetic to their *female* children. They usually included uppercase and lowercase alphabet(s), numbers, and the name of the child and the date the sampler was stitched.

The sampler was often very ornate, with many different embroidery stitches and designs included to teach the child different techniques.

This is the simplest example of a teaching sampler. It was worked in Cross-Stitch (see page 45) and Back-stitch (see page 94). The design area is 57 stitches × 92 stitches.

*Note: The outline of a rose was used in place of the name Rose in this sampler.*

## MATERIALS

Zweigart® #14 Aida (10″ × 12″)

DMC® Floss, #666 (3-ply, 1 skein), #814 (1 ply, 1 skein), **Green for leaves** (3-ply, 18″), and **Red or pink for rose** (2-ply, 18″)

#26 tapestry needle

## PREPARATION

**1.** Hem all sides of the fabric to prevent raveling.

**2.** Mark center lines on fabric (horizontal and vertical) with a basting thread.

**3.** Photocopy or copy the letters of the alphabet (Alphabet #4, page 184) to make the name of the child. Paste up as shown on the diagram.

## TO WORK

**1.** Using Cross-Stitch, follow the diagram for the placement of the alphabet letters and the name.

**2.** *Do not forget to date the work.*

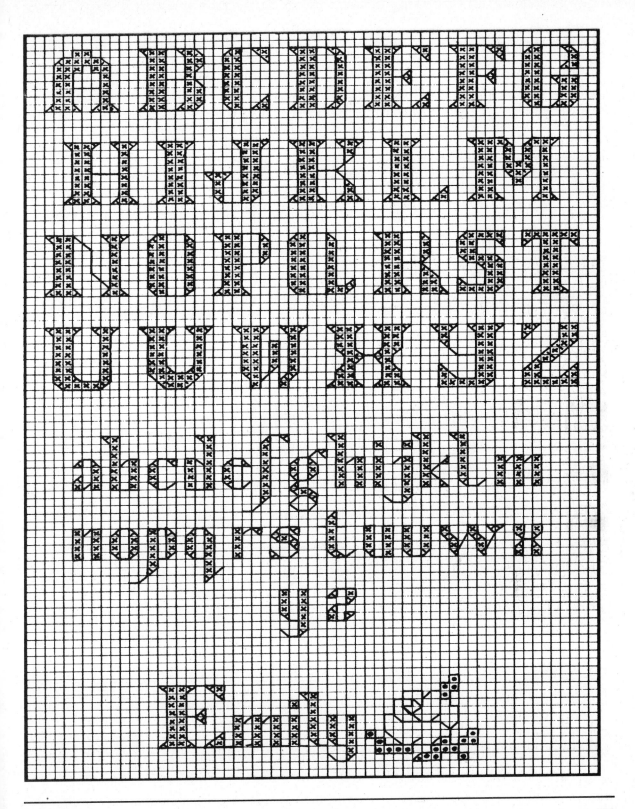

# NAPKIN RINGS

Napkin rings are an easy-to-make embellishment for your dinner table. When I have a large group for a holiday dinner, I use napkin rings as place cards so that each person will know where I would like her or him to sit. Then I give each person the napkin ring to take home as a gift from me.

## MATERIALS

Ribband® by Bucilla® or Zweigart® Stitchband #7107 (6″ long)

DMC® Floss in any color (use 1 strand)

#26 tapestry needle

Emily Rose Sampler Alphabet (see page 184)

## PREPARATION

1. Cut 6″ length of edged fabric.

2. Fold fabric in half lengthwise and short edge to short edge to find the center; mark center with a pin or basting thread.

3. Using Emily Rose Sampler Alphabet, copy a name or initials onto graph paper.

## TO WORK

1. Work Cross-Stitches following your own diagram and centered on the fabric. I have included the 3 diagrams used for the 3 samples.

**Note:** *Diagram A ("jason") was worked with 1 strand of DMC® #666 over 1 fabric thread.*

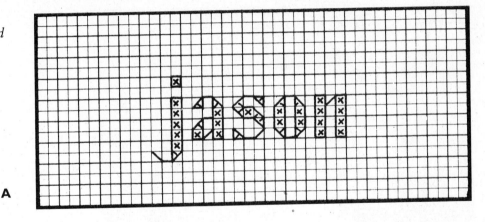

**A**

*Diagram B ("ryan") was worked with 2 strands over 2 fabric threads. It was outlined with 1 strand using Backstitches.*

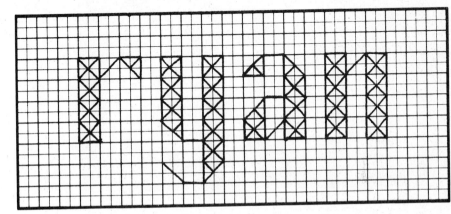

**B**

*Diagram C ("Emily Rose") was worked with 1 strand of DMC® #666 for the name Emily (in Cross-Stitch) and 1 strand each of #905 and #604 for the outline of the rose.*

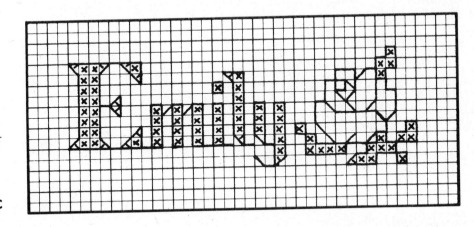

**C**

## FINISHING

1. Fold in half with right sides facing and seam across the short end, ½" from the edge.

2. With pinking shears, cut the sewn edge ¼" from the seam line. Press and turn right side out.

# BLACKWORK BORDER TOWEL

## MATERIALS

Charles Craft check towel with #14 Aida border

DMC® Floss #310 Black (18″)

DMC® Perle Cotton #8 (1 spool)

#24 tapestry needle

Emily Rose Sampler Alphabet (see page 184)

Blackwork Pattern #6 (see page 22)

Hoop

## PREPARATION

**1.** Using the Emily Rose Sampler Alphabet, choose 1 initial. I added 2 horizontal rows to the diagram to make the initial 10 fabric threads high. This can easily be done for any letter, or the alphabet can be used as diagrammed (8 fabric threads high).

**2.** Baste a center line (horizontal and vertical) on the Aida border band.

## TO WORK

1. Using 3 strands of DMC® Floss #310, work the chosen initial in the center of the Aida border band with Cross-Stitches (see page 45).

2. Using DMC® Perle Cotton #8, stitch Blackwork Pattern #6. I have used my initial on the sample with the Blackwork around it to show the placement around the initial. Use the Holbein Stitch (see page 129) to make the Blackwork reversible.

3. Extend all rows of Blackwork to each side edge.

CENTER

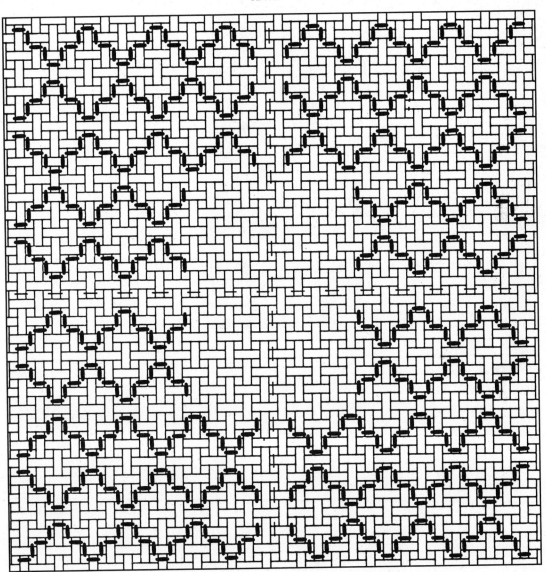

# PULLED-THREAD ALPHABET TOWEL

Pulled-Thread stitches are not usually worked on Aida Cloth. However, with experimentation I found that stitches requiring no pull or medium pull can not only be worked on Aida but give a beautiful effect, as shown on the sample.

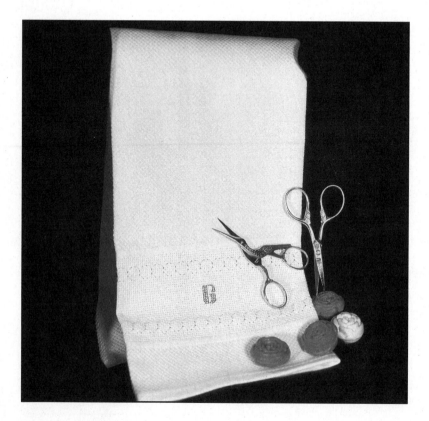

## MATERIALS

**Charles Craft Huck towel with #14 Aida border insert**

**DMC® Perle Cotton #8 Ecru** (8 yards)

**DMC® Floss #644** (3-ply, 1 yard)

**Kreinik Blending Hi Lustre Antique Gold** (1 yard)

**Emily Rose Sampler** Alphabet (see page 184)

## PREPARATION

**1.** Choose initial(s) from the Emily Rose Sampler Alphabet. There is enough room on the front of the folded towel for 1 to 6 letters.

**2.** Make a basting line both across and down the middle of the Aida insert.

## TO WORK

**1.** Using #8 Perle Cotton and starting in the center, 6 horizontal threads down from the top of the Aida insert, work a *complete* row of Ringed Back-stitch (see page 138). Then work the other side of the center until you have a finished border of Ringed Backstitch.

**2.** Repeat across the bottom edge of the Aida insert, remembering to leave 6 unworked horizontal fabric threads.

**3.** Using 3 strands of #644 Floss and 1 strand of Antique Gold, work your chosen initials in the center of the Aida band.

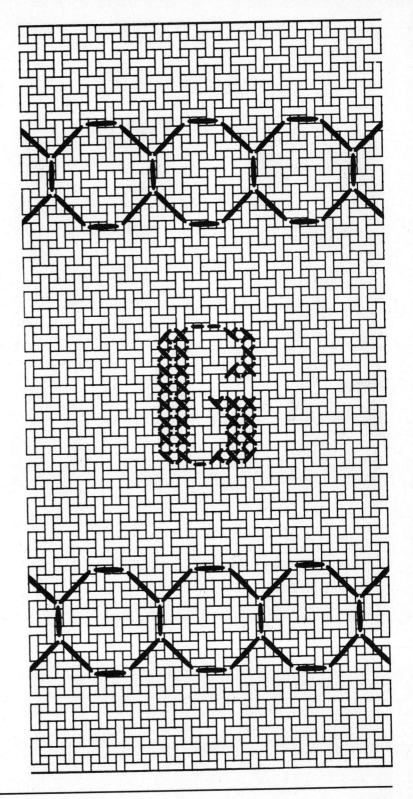

# EYELET ALPHABET TOWEL

Here is an example of another pulled stitch used successfully on an Aida evenweave insert.

## MATERIALS

Charles Craft KitchenMates hang towel

DMC® Floss #3609 (1 skein)

Kreinik Silver Cable (about 2 yards)

Eyelet Alphabet (see page 181)

## PREPARATION

1. Using the Eyelet Alphabet and the diagram as your guide, copy (or photocopy and paste up) your chosen name.

2. Baste a center line down and across the center of the Aida band.

## TO WORK

1. Using 3 strands of DMC® Floss #3609 (or another color of your choice) work the Backstitches (or you may use Holbein Stitches; see page 129 according to the diagram). Leave space for the Eyelet Stitches.

2. Using Kreinik Silver Cable (1-ply, as it comes from the spool), work the Eyelet Stitches as shown on the diagram.

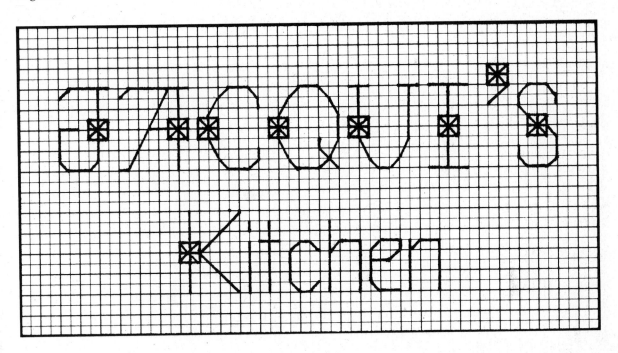

# CHESS ANYONE?

This wonderful piece of Blackwork embroidery was designed and stitched by Dale Sokolow as a current Embroiderers' Guild of America Group Correspondence Course.

I have included this chessboard to show that beautiful embroidery can be a *"work of art."*

For information about the Embroiderers' Guild of America and directions for this Group Correspondence Course, you can contact the EGA at 335 West Broadway, Suite 100, Louisville, KY 40202-4122, or telephone (502) 589-6956.

# Alphabets

Some of the projects require you to work alphabets or individual letters for monograms or for signing your work.

## ALPHABET #1 (ASSISI)

The sample is worked on Zweigart® Aida #14 with DMC® #8 Perle Cotton for the black outline and DMC® Cotton Floss #666 for the Cross-Stitches.

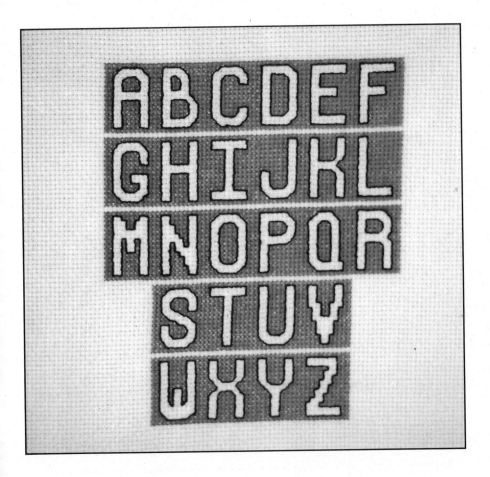

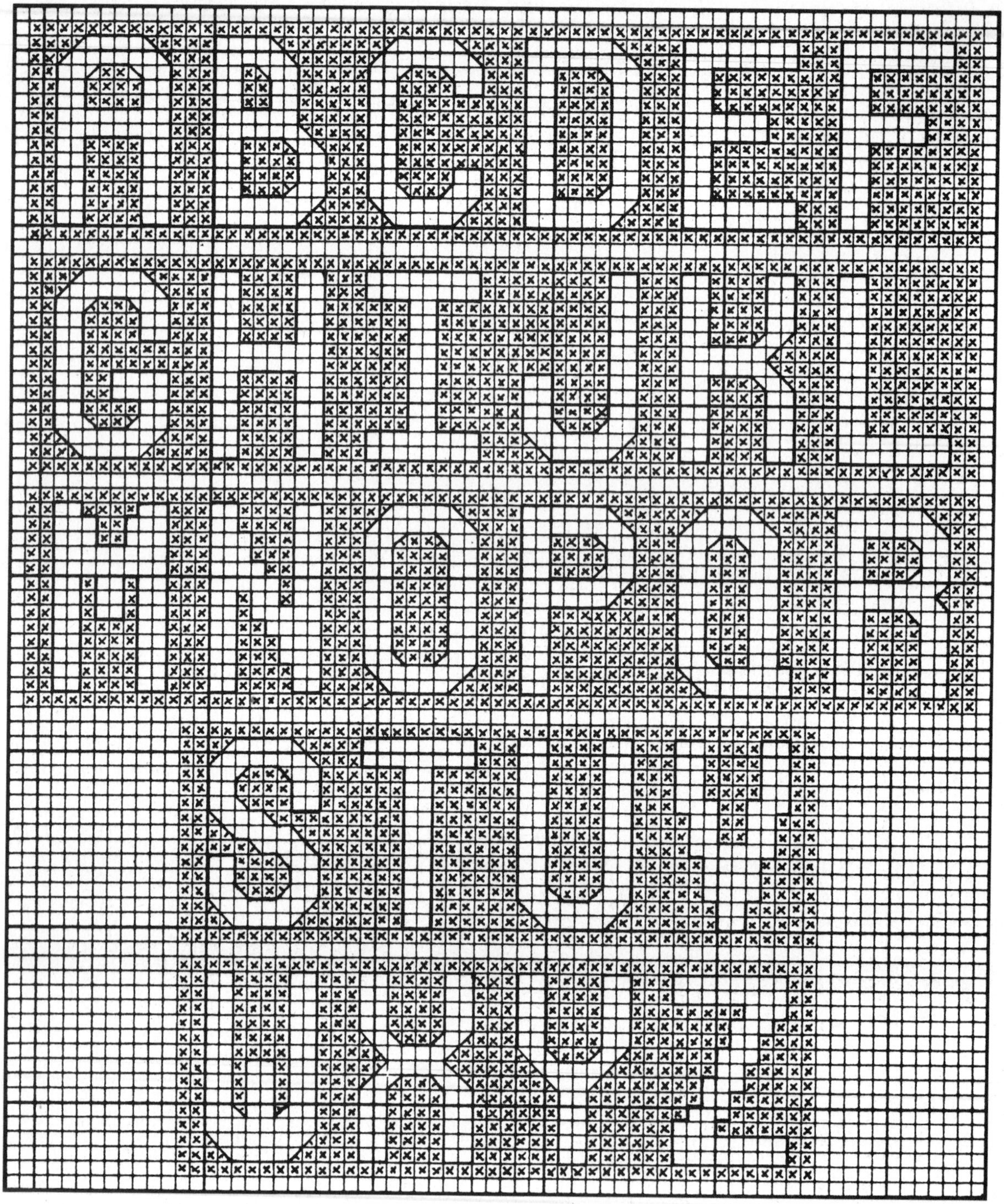

# ALPHABET #2 (WITH EYELET STITCHES, UPPERCASE AND LOWERCASE)

The sample is worked on Zweigart® Aida #18 with DMC® Cotton Floss (2-ply) and Kreinik Balger Cable Gold.

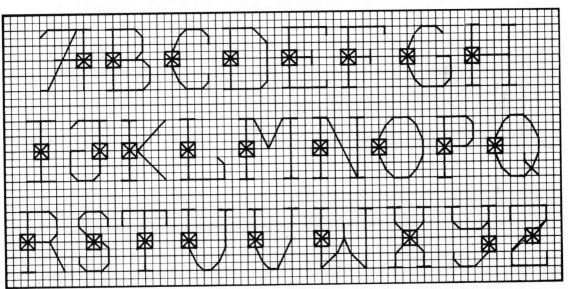

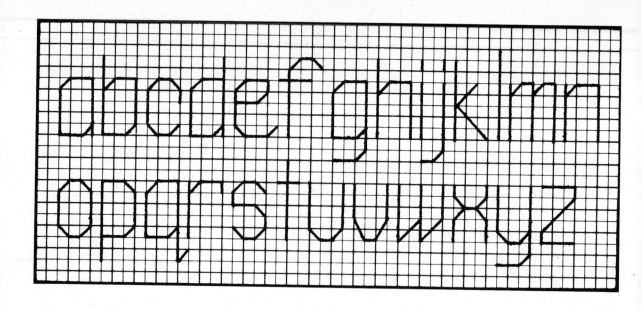

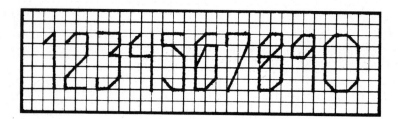

# ALPHABET #3 (JOINED LETTERS, UPPERCASE, LOWERCASE, AND NUMBERS)

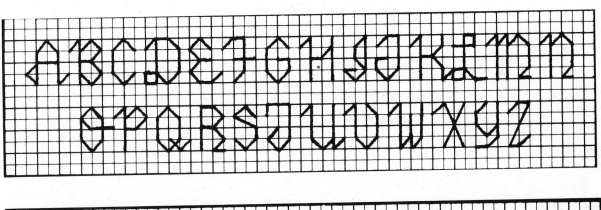

The sample is worked on Zweigart®
Aida #14 with DMC® Cotton Floss.

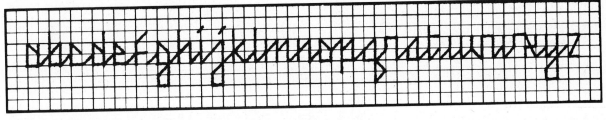

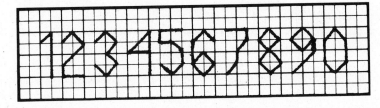

# ALPHABET #4 (EMILY ROSE SAMPLER ALPHABET, UPPERCASE AND LOWERCASE)

The sample is worked on Zweigart® #28 Brittany with DMC® Cotton Floss.

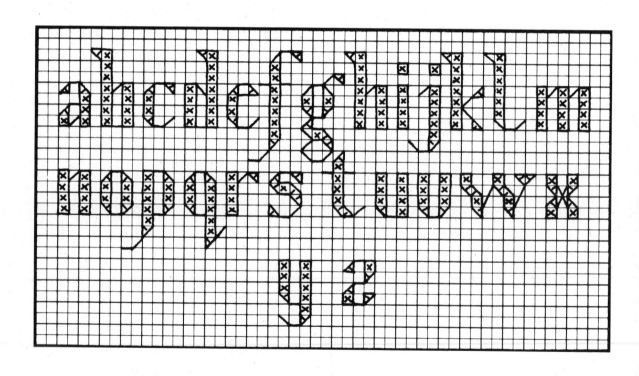

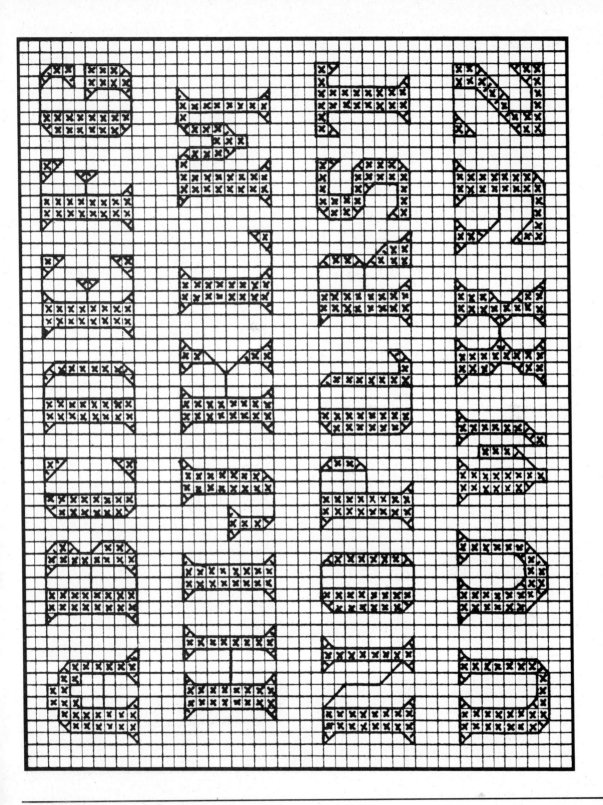

# ALPHABET #6 (DARNING PATTERN ALPHABET)

The alphabet pattern was designed to fit the Darning Pattern Border Towel project (see page 166). Of course, it can be used for many other projects.

# Finishing Touches

When a design is worked with hours of careful planning and stitching, it deserves fine finishing. You can have it framed, wear it, or display it in some other way. Any method you choose must be done carefully and neatly. If you can do it yourself, great. If you cannot, please choose your professional framer or finisher with care.

*Note: For the less adventuresome stitcher or those who want an instant finished product, a number of manufacturers have produced well-finished soft goods to be embroidered. Charles Craft supplied the lovely towels used in this book. They may be seen in the chapter "Projects" (pages 152 to 178).*

## CLEANING

Oil from your hands, marks from hoop rings, and other types of soil are often left on the embroidered piece and *must* be removed before any finishing or framing can be considered.

Most needlework fabrics and threads can be hand-washed. You can test the fabric or threads for color-fastness by washing a scrap piece. If you are not sure of the fabric used, or if the threads run, place your work in the hands of a professional dry cleaner.

### TO WASH

**1.** Dissolve a mild soap (like Ivory Flakes)—or a *specialty* product made to remove soil marks and body oils from needlework—in cool water.

**2.** Add the stitched work and let it soak for 5 to 10 minutes. Then gently squeeze the suds through the fabric.

**3.** Rinse well in cold water.

**4.** *Never twist or wring the fabric.* Place the embroidered piece on a clean towel, cover with another clean towel, and roll up to remove excess water.

**5.** Place the work on another clean, dry towel on a flat surface and allow to damp-dry. Do not place it in the sun or near a source of artificial heat.

**6.** You can press the needlework on the *wrong* side until it is smooth and dry.

# Index of Stitches